MW00398634

a-**MAIZE**-*ing*

tailgating

a-**MAIZE**-*ing* *tailgating*

Wolverine Cuisine

compiled by
Suzanne Wangler

Printed in Canada

99 98 97 3 2 1

Momentum Books, Ltd.
6964 Crooks Rd.
Troy, Michigan 48098

Edited by Tom Seller
Cover Art by Gino Danelli
Photographs by permission of Bob Kalmbach, Philip Dattilo, the Schembechler family and Michigan Sports Information Services.
All material in the Halftime Entertainment section by permission of *Michigan Alumnus* magazine and the Michigan Alumni Association.

ISBN: 1-879094-54-1

Library of Congress Cataloging-in-Publication Data

A-maize-ing tailgating : Wolverine cuisine / compiled by Suzanne Wangler.
p. cm.
Includes index.
ISBN 1-879094-54-1 (v. 1 : alk. paper)
1. Cookery, American. 2. Tailgate parties. 3. Michigan Wolverines (Football team) I. Wangler, Suzanne, 1964– . II. University of Michigan
TX715.A5074 1997
641.5973--dc21 97-17673

Printed in Canada

To the memory of Millie Schembechler
for all her love and support
of the University of Michigan and
its football program

Definitions

football : a game played with a football on a rectangular field having two goalposts by two teams whose object is to get the ball over the goal line

food : material containing or consisting of carbohydrates, fats, proteins and supplementary substances used to sustain growth, vital processes and to furnish energy

drink : a liquid suitable for swallowing

tailgate : a gate at the rear of a vehicle that can be let down for loading and unloading

a-maize-ing tailgating : an unusually congenial combination of all of the above, carried on at Michigan Stadium

Contents

1st Quarter—Snacks, Dips, and Spreads

Preface

Funny—a Buckeye compiling a cookbook for Wolverine fans! (Hint: you'd better double-check all the recipes to make sure they taste OK.) Just kidding!

In case you are wondering, this cookbook is the brainchild of Teresa Wangler, aka Mama Wangs. Teresa is the mother of John Wangler, quarterback for the University of Michigan from 1978 to 1981. If the name sounds familiar, John happens to be my husband. (See what happens on a blind date in Columbus...a Wolverine and a Buckeye connect and ta-daaa! a cookbook.)

Back to Mama Wangs. Her recipes for Cincinnati chili, spinach square, and Texas sheet cake are known throughout the Big Ten. Teresa and her cast of tailgating characters have been stationed at UM Victor's lot for the past twenty years. No tailgate is complete without tasting her latest creations.

So, after years of sharing secret recipes and trying out new ones, Teresa came up with the idea of compiling everyone's favorite recipes.

Well, Teresa had the idea. I offered to do the legwork, and John suggested we dedicate the cookbook to the memory of Millie Schembechler, the First Lady of Michigan football. Thus *a-MAIZE-ing tailgating* was born.

Millie, for those of you who might not know, is the late wife of former UM head football coach Bo Schembechler. Just as Teresa is known far and wide for her recipes, Millie will best be remembered for her love and support of the UM football program. And don't get me wrong; her four boys as well as Bo say she was one heck of a cook!

Bo and Millie also met on a blind date—and married in 1968. In 1979, Millie took on a big project at the University of Michigan. She researched the first 100 years of Michigan football. Millie collected and set up an exhibit of memorabilia in Crisler Arena. From that time she continued to be involved with local alumni and service-oriented groups.

In early 1992, tragedy struck the Schembechler home. Millie was diagnosed with adrenal cancer. The diagnosis came suddenly. This type of cancer is so rare it affects only two people per million. Millie put up quite a fight, but the cancer took her life on August 19, 1992. Millie was just sixty-three years old.

In the wake of Millie's death, Bo decided to try to win a big battle for his beloved wife—to fight this rare form of cancer. Through the University of Michigan Bo helped set up the Millie Schembechler Adrenal Cancer Fund. Through fund-raisers, awareness programs, and events, such as the Millie Schembechler Golf Outing every summer, Bo tries to raise money for the foundation. The money helps doctors try to determine what causes adrenal cancer, and how to treat it.

After talking with Bo, another decision was made—proceeds would go to the Millie Schembechler Adrenal Cancer Fund at the University of Michigan Medical Center.

Acknowledgments

I want to thank all Millie's close friends for sharing their favorite Millie stories. My thanks to all the true-blue coaches, players, and media types who mailed and faxed their favorite recipes in record time.

I also want to thank all the people who helped put this book together. All the folks from the University of Michigan who helped with trivia, pictures, and player information without their help this book truly wouldn't be as "a-maize-ing." A special thanks to Kyle Scott at Momentum Books. And thanks to my family for all their love and support.

With all that said, what else can I say (and you know how tough this is for a Buckeye) but, hey...GO BLUE!

First Quarter
Snacks, Dips and Spreads

Cold Pizza

Bo Schembechler (Millie's)

1 package crescent rolls
8 ounces cream cheese
1 cup mayonnaise
1 teaspoon dill weed
1 tablespoon onions (cut up)

Toppings
chopped tomatoes
sprouts
green peppers
mushrooms
Parmesan cheese

Press rolls in pan till thin. Bake at 400° for 10 minutes and cool. Mix cream cheese, mayonnaise, dill weed, and onions. Carefully spread over cooked rolls. Add toppings as desired, any combination. Put in refrigerator for 4-6 hours before serving.

Bo Schembechler—Michigan's head football coach from 1969 to 1990, earned 13 conference championships in his 22 seasons. He finished as the winningest head coach in Michigan football history with 194 victories. Schembechler came to Michigan from Miami of Ohio, where he coached from 1963 to 1968.

Bean Dip

Bo Schembechler (Millie's)

1 16-ounce can refried beans
1 package taco seasoning
½ jar salsa
1 pint sour cream
black olives
green onions
1 package shredded cheese

Combine refried beans, ½ package taco seasoning, and salsa and mix well. Spread in pan or cookie sheet. Mix rest of taco seasoning with sour cream. Spread on top of bean mixture. Top with green onions and olives and cheese. Add any toppings that you like. Serve with tortilla chips.

Oyster Crackers

President Gerald Ford

- *1 bottle Redenbacher's butter-flavored popcorn oil*
- *2 12-ounce packages oyster crackers (Sunshine or Nabisco)*
- *2 packages Hidden Valley Original Ranch Dressing mix*
- *¼ teaspoon lemon pepper*
- *¼ teaspoon garlic powder*
- *¼ teaspoon dill*

Place crackers in roasting pan. Mix all other ingredients together and pour over crackers. Mix well. Bake at 350° for 6 minutes, stirring every 2 minutes. Cool.

At the 2-minute intervals, stir crackers well with a wide spatula, getting as much of the oil off the bottom of the pan as possible. After the third stirring, the oil should have been absorbed by the crackers. The crackers can be put in freezer bags and frozen.

Gerald Ford—The center and MVP of Michigan's 1934 team, Ford also saw action as a member of Michigan's 1932 and 1933 national championship teams. The Grand Rapids native was named an honorable mention all-Big Ten choice in 1934.

Beef Puffs

Ray Lane

Puffs

- 2 *tablespoons butter or margarine*
- ¼ *cup boiling water*
- ¼ *cup flour*
- *dash salt*
- 1 *egg*
- ¼ *cup shredded Swiss cheese*

Melt butter or margarine in boiling water. Add flour and salt; stir vigorously. Cook and stir till mixture forms a ball that doesn't separate. Remove from heat and cool slightly. Add the egg, and beat vigorously till smooth. Stir in Swiss cheese. Drop dough onto greased baking sheet, using 1 level teaspoon for each puff. Bake at 400° about 20 minutes. Remove from oven, split, and cool.

Filling

- 1 *3½-ounce package thin sliced beef (finely snipped)*
- ⅓ *cup finely chopped celery*
- 2 *tablespoons chopped green pepper*
- 1 *teaspoon horseradish*
- ⅓ *cup mayonnaise*

Combine all ingredients. Chill. Spoon into puffs just before serving. Arrange tops.

Ray Lane—Ray has spent a majority of his broadcast career following UM at WJBK-TV and WKBD-TV as sports director.

Cheese Onion Bread

Bob Trimble (Kim's)

1 loaf frozen bread dough
½ cup (1 stick) butter or margarine, melted
pinch dry or Dijon mustard
2 tablespoons poppy seeds
1 large onion, chopped
1 tablespoon Morton's Nature's Seasons Blend seasoning
lemon juice to taste
1 8-ounce package sliced mozzarella cheese
1 8-ounce package sliced Swiss cheese

Thaw dough according to package directions. When risen, turn onto a cookie sheet and shape dough into a rectangle like French bread. Bake at 375° for 15 minutes. Combine remaining ingredients and set aside. Remove bread from oven and cut slices halfway through about 1" apart. *Do not cut all the way through.* Fold a slice of mozzarella and Swiss cheese together and place into each cut. Brush the butter mixture generously over the bread. Continue baking at 375° for another 15 minutes. Finish slicing through each cut into individual pieces.

Note: this is a favorite recipe of our family, especially in the summer, with any barbecued meat or poultry. It's very easy to prepare ahead of time, wrap in foil, and take with you anywhere.

Bob Trimble is a sportscaster for WKBD-TV in Detroit.

Tapenade Spread

Andrea Joyce

- *¼ cup olive oil*
- *2 cups sliced onions*
- *½ cup chopped sun-dried tomatoes (oil cured; drained)*
- *½ cup chopped Kalamata olives (or more to taste)*
- *fresh baguettes slices*

Sauté onions in olive oil on medium-low heat until dark brown. Place onions, tomatoes, and olives in food processor; use on-off switch to make a chunky paste. Season with pepper. Can be refrigerated for a week. Serve at room temperature.

Andrea Joyce—The CBS Sports Anchor/Reporter has been at the network since 1989 covering a variety of sporting events. But little do viewers know she got her first taste of college sports at the University of Michigan. This UM alum spent several years covering the Wolverines during her stint at WDIV-TV, Detroit. Andrea is currently the host of "At the Half" and the "CBS Sports Show". She is a Detroit, Michigan, native now living with her husband Harry Smith and their two boys in New York.

Crab Dip

Pete Elliott

8 ounces cream cheese
½ cup seafood cocktail sauce
horseradish
Tabasco
1 6-ounce can crabmeat

Soften cream cheese and add cocktail sauce. Mix well. Add a little horseradish and Tabasco to taste. Drain liquid off crabmeat and add to cheese. Serve with plain crackers.

Pete Elliott—A 1948 all-American quarterback who led Michigan to a national championship. Elliott is the only athlete to win 12 letters at Michigan, earning them in football, basketball, and golf. A member of four championship teams, Elliott became a head coach at Nebraska, California, and Illinois.

Shrimp Dip

Lloyd Carr

- 2 *large packages cream cheese, softened*
- 2 *cans tiny shrimp*
- ¾ *bottle chili sauce*
- ½ *onion, minced*
- ½ *teaspoon lemon juice*
- 2 *shakes Worcestershire sauce*
- 2 *tablespoons horseradish (optional)*

Mix together and refrigerate for at least an hour.

Lloyd Carr—Michigan's head football coach, Carr has spent the past 21 years in collegiate coaching, the last 17 with the Wolverines. In 1980 Carr started as UM's defensive backs coach, progressing to defensive coordinator in 1987 and assistant head coach in 1990. In 1995 he was named Michigan's seventeenth head coach.

Spiced Pecans

Joe Roberson

¾ stick of butter
1 egg white
1 cup sugar
½ teaspoon salt
¼ teaspoon cinnamon
¼ teaspoon cloves
¼ teaspoon allspice
1 pound pecans

Heat oven to 300°. Melt butter in a 9" x 13" pan and set aside. Beat egg white until stiff. In a separate bowl, mix sugar, salt, cinnamon, cloves, and allspice. Stir mixture into egg white (mixture will be stiff; you can divide it). Add pecans to sugar and spices and coat. Add coated pecans to melted butter and spread evenly. Bake 50 minutes. Stir twice during cooking. Remove to paper towel-lined cookie sheet.

Joe Roberson—Joe is the University of Michigan's 8th athletic director. He has been associated with the maize and blue in some capacity since he received his undergraduate degree from the University of Michigan-Flint. Besides standing out in the business world, he was one heck of an athlete himself. Roberson enjoyed a stellar basketball and baseball career. He signed as a left-handed pitcher with the Brooklyn Dodgers in 1953. Since his days on the field, Roberson now takes time to make sure they're running smoothly for the Wolverines off the field as the a.d.

Braunschweiger Ball

Bill McCartney

3 *pounds braunschweiger*
6 *packages green-onion dip mix*
3 *teaspoons sugar*
6 *teaspoons water*
18 *ounce packages cream cheese*
3 *tablespoons milk*
¼ *teaspoon hot pepper sauce*
2 *2¼-ounce ripe olives, chopped*
3 *tablespoons garlic spread*
sprinkle of chives

Mash up braunschweiger and combine with dip mix, sugar, water, and olives; form into ball shape. Soften garlic spread and whip with other ingredients to make a spread to cover the outside of the ball; sprinkle with chives.

Bill McCartney—A Michigan assistant coach under Bo Schembechler from 1974 to 1981, McCartney coached the linebackers and moved to defensive coordinator in his eight seasons, during which Michigan won five Big Ten titles. McCartney now heads a men's organization called the Promise Keepers.

Hommus Dip (Chickpea Dip)

Mike Leoni

1 pound can chickpeas
juice of 2 lemons
3 medium cloves garlic, chopped
1 teaspoon salt, or to taste
⅓ cup tahini (sesame seed oil)
3 tablespoons water

Boil chickpeas on low heat for 15 minutes in their own juices. Drain. In a food processor or blender put lemon juice, garlic, salt, tahini, chickpeas, and part water. Blend on low. Stir with rubber spatula. Blend on medium or high, adding water for desired thickness; at this point also taste for salt and lemon. Serve in a bowl and garnish with paprika and chopped parsley. Sprinkle olive oil on top if desired. Refrigerate. Delicious dipped with Syrian bread.

Note: more lemon is better.

Mike Leoni—Mike played offensive tackle from 1976 to 1980. The Leoni family is known throughout the Big Ten for their lavish, legendary tailgates in their motor home. Mike resides in Saline, Michigan, with his wife and two potential first-round-draft-pick sons.

Michigan Go Blue Dip

Bubba Paris

juice of half a lemon
2 *teaspoons powdered mustard*
½ *teaspoon Tabasco sauce*
½ *teaspoon seasoned salt*
½ *teaspoon black pepper*
½ *cup mayonnaise*
3 *tablespoons chopped onions*
4 *ounces cream cheese*
3 *whole cooked eggs (no shells, please)*

Blend with a mixer lemon juice, powdered mustard, Tabasco sauce, seasoned salt, black pepper, and mayonnaise. Add onions and cream cheese. Mix eggs in blender and add to above. Serve on crackers.

Spicy Salsa

Bubba Paris

1 medium red onion, minced
5 ripe red tomatoes, peeled, seeded, and chopped coarsely
2 hot jalapeños, seeded and minced finely
2 bunches cilantro, stemmed and chopped
⅓ cup lime juice
1 cup virgin olive oil

Mix together and enjoy!

Bubba Paris—An all-American tackle and two-time all-Big Ten pick for Michigan between 1978 and 1981. Started 33 games in his collegiate career before being drafted in the second round by the San Francisco 49ers. Played in three NFL Super Bowls.

Hot Wings and Dip

Reggie McKenzie

12 wings (about 2 pounds)
2 tablespoons butter
2-3 teaspoons hot pepper sauce
1 teaspoon paprika

Clean wings, cut tips, place in shallow baking pan.

Stir melted butter, hot pepper sauce, paprika; pour over wings. Let marinate at room temperature 30 minutes. Drain chicken; save sauce. Brush chicken with sauce. Broil 4″-5″ from heat 10 minutes or until it burns a bit, then repeat on other side.

Blue Cheese Dip
½ cup sour cream
½ cup mayonnaise
½ cup crumbled blue cheese
1 clove minced garlic
1 tablespoon white wine vinegar

Blend together ingredients and top with crumbled blue cheese.

Reggie McKenzie—An all-American choice at guard in 1971, McKenzie was part of two Big Ten Champion and Rose Bowl teams during his career. The two-time all-Big Ten selection played 12 years in the NFL after his outstanding Michigan career.

Cheese and Olive Canapés

Reggie McKenzie

1 ½ cups Hellman's mayonnaise
½ cup onion, finely chopped
1 ½ cups sharp cheese, shredded
1 cup black olives, chopped
1 teaspoon curry powder
½ teaspoon salt
8 halves English muffins, toasted

Mix ingredients and pile on split toasted English muffins. Cut in quarters. Put under broiler briefly, just until they sizzle and sear hot.

Spinach Dip

Chris Calloway

- *1 10-ounce package frozen chopped spinach, boiled and drained*
- *1 box Knorr vegetable soup mix*
- *1 can water chestnuts, chopped*
- *1 medium onion, chopped*
- *1 cup mayonnaise*
- *1⅓ cups sour cream*
- *1 round loaf of bread*

Cut off the top of the bread and cut out the inside, leaving a shell. Mix all ingredients together and put into the round bread shell. Cut or tear the bread that was removed into bite-size pieces. Use these pieces to dip.

Chris Calloway—During his three years at UM, Calloway caught 56 passes for 826 yards. The Chicago, Illinois, native grabbed eight touchdown receptions and played in two Rose Bowls before playing professionally with the New York Giants.

Hot Chili Dip

Stephan Humphries

1 can of "no beans" chili
2 pounds Velveeta cheese
3 jalapeño peppers
1 medium onion, chopped

Put all ingredients in a bowl and microwave, mixing occasionally, till blended. Use as a dip for crackers or tortilla chips.

Stephan Humphries—Offensive guard. Best noted as one of the top linemen to ever wear the maize and blue. He was a leader on and off the field. He captained the 1983 squad that played in the Sugar Bowl and was twice picked as academic all-American. He was also awarded the Big Ten conference's "medal of honor" for excellence in academics and athletics. He was a two-time first team all-Big Ten selection. He was drafted by the Chicago Bears.

Shrimp Log

Anthony Carter

1 8-ounce package cream cheese, softened
1 cup minced cooked shrimp
2 tablespoons chili sauce
2 tablespoons chopped green onion
1 teaspoon lemon juice
2 tablespoons chopped stuffed olives
sliced stuffed olives

In a bowl, stir cream cheese until smooth. Blend in cooked shrimp, chili sauce, olives, onion, and lemon juice. Shape into a log and garnish with sliced stuffed olives. Chill thoroughly. Serve with crackers.

Anthony Carter—A native of Riviera Beach, Florida, Carter was a three-time all-American and three-time all-Big Ten pick at wide receiver for Michigan. After a four-year UM career that saw him break every receiving record in the Michigan record books, Carter embarked on a 13-year professional football career. He finished fourth in the Heisman Trophy voting in 1982.

Pizza Fondue

Ali Haji-Sheikh

- 1 *onion, chopped*
- 1 *pound ground chuck*
- 2 *(10½-ounce each) cans pizza sauce*
- 1 *tablespoon cornstarch*
- 1½ *teaspoons oregano*
- ¼ *teaspoon garlic powder*
- 10 *ounces cheddar cheese*
- 1 *cup mozzarella cheese*

Brown onions and ground chuck. Add rest of ingredients except mozzarella cheese. Heat; add mozzarella cheese just before serving. Serve with toasted English muffins cut into bite-size pieces or tortilla chips.

Ali Haji-Sheikh—Served as the placekicker for UM from 1979 to 1982, converting 31 field goals and 117 extra points in his four seasons. After being named second team all-Big Ten in 1982, Haji-Sheikh went on to play with the New York Giants and set the NFL record for field goals in a season in 1983.

Zucchini Pancakes

Mel Owens

- 1 *large zucchini*
- 2 *eggs*
- ½ *cup Parmesan cheese*
- *parsley*
- *garlic salt*
- ¼ *cup flour*
- *milk*
- *salt*

Grate zucchini, add a dash of salt, and let stand. Beat eggs, add cheese, parsley, garlic salt, and milk. Squeeze the zucchini until most of the water is gone. Mix with egg mixture and add flour. This mixture will resemble potato pancake mixture. Fry in hot oil until golden brown.

Mel Owens—A 1980 all-Big Ten selection, Owens started at linebacker in the 1981 Rose Bowl. He started 23 games in his three-year career and played on two Big Ten Champion squads.

Stuffed Mushrooms

Thomas Seabron

- 12 *large mushrooms*
- 2 *tablespoons butter*
- 1 *medium onion*
- ½ *cup pepperoni, grated*
- ¼ *cup grated green onion*
- ½ *teaspoon basil*
- ½ *cup Ritz crackers, crushed*
- 3 *tablespoons Parmesan cheese*
- 1 *tablespoon parsley flakes*
- ½ *teaspoon seasoned salt*
- ¼ *teaspoon oregano*
- ⅛ *teaspoon pepper*
- ½ *cup chicken broth*
- 1 *small clove garlic*

Melt butter in pan and sauté onion, pepperoni, green onion, garlic, and chopped mushroom stems. Add the rest of the ingredients and sauté for five more minutes. Set aside to cool. Carefully stuff the stemless mushrooms with the cooled mixture. Bake at 350° for 12 minutes.

Thomas Seabron—The Detroit native played four years for the Wolverines (1975–78) and was part of three conference championships. The outside linebacker started 10 of 12 games during the 1978 campaign.

Smoked Go Bluefish

Jim Harbaugh

- *3 smoked bluefish cooked and chopped*
- *1 8-ounce package cream cheese*
- *1 cup heavy cream*
- *dash Tabasco*
- *dash horseradish*
- *1 teaspoon margarine*

Mix and serve on crackers.

Jim Harbaugh—An outstanding quarterback, Harbaugh led the Wolverines to a Big Ten title in 1985 and a Fiesta Bowl victory in 1986. The nation's most efficient passer in 1985, he went on to set several school passing records. He received Michigan's MVP, Big Ten Player of the Year, and came in third in voting for the Heisman Trophy. He continues his passing excellence as the starting quarterback for the Indianapolis Colts.

Dixon's Graham Stix

Tom Dixon

- 2 *sticks of "I Can't Believe It's Not Butter"*
- ½ *cup sugar*
- 8 *ounces graham crackers*
- 1 *cup chopped pecans*

Bring butter and sugar to a slow boil (boil 2 minutes only!). Break graham crackers at seams, to make them look like sticks. Pour butter and sugar mixture over graham sticks. Sprinkle with chopped pecans and bake at 350° for 10 minutes.

Tom Dixon, center—Dixon was instrumental to the great Michigan running teams of the early 1980s. He was the center on two Big Ten championship squads and named to the UPI and Kodak all-American teams in 1983. He started every game of his last three seasons. He was also a standout in the classroom. He posted a 3.27 GPA as a pre-med student. He was named to several Big Ten and all-American academic teams.

Dutchess of Windsor Appetizer

Ernie Harwell (Lulu's)

½ pound bacon
½ cup chopped green onion
¼ cup mayonnaise
24 toast rounds (wheat melba or rye melba)

Fry bacon till crisp. (I usually microwave it with paper towel over and under it.) Drain and crumble. Combine bacon, onion, and mayonnaise. Blend. Spread one tablespoon on each toast round. Heat in oven at 350° till bubbles. Very good!

Ernie Harwell was the "Voice of Tiger Baseball" for over 30 years. He is in the Baseball Hall of Fame.

Mama Wang's Spinach Squares

John Wangler

- 4 *tablespoons butter, melted*
- 1 *egg*
- 1 *cup flour*
- 1 *cup milk*
- 1 *teaspoon salt*
- 1 *tablespoon baking powder*
- 1 *medium grated onion*
- ½ *pound cheddar cheese*
- ½ *pound Monterey Jack cheese*
- 2 *10-ounce packages frozen chopped spinach, thawed and drained*

Mix flour, egg, milk, salt, baking powder; add remaining ingredients.

Note: the butter does not go into the recipe, but it is melted at the bottom of the baking pan. After melted butter is placed into bottom of pan, add the spinach mixture over it.

Bake at 350° for 35 minutes, cool, cut, and serve.

John Wangler—Michigan's leader in passing yardage in 1979 and in 1980, Wangler threw for 145 yards in delivering the Wolverines their first Rose Bowl win in 16 years in 1981. Though he played only two years, Wangler still ranks seventh in Michigan's all-time passing yardage leaders and sixth in touchdown passes thrown.

Spicy Dipping Sauce

Don Coleman

1 egg, beaten
2 tablespoons Chinese barbecue sauce (satay paste)
1 tablespoon soy sauce

Mix all ingredients together. Great with chicken wings or even vegetables

Don Coleman—Defensive end in 1972 and 1973. He had 114 career tackles and 2 career interceptions. This football standout from the West Coast started 21 games at right end. He also played on two Big Ten championship teams.

Stuffed Cherry Tomatoes

Dan Dickerson

- 1 *smal bunch parsley, chopped fine*
- 1 *small bunch of scallions, chopped fine (green tops only)*
- ½ *cup bulgar wheat (soaked in cold water for 1 hour then drained)*
- ½ *cup canned tomatoes (include juice)*
- *juice of 2 lemons*
- 3 *tablespoons olive oil*
- 24 *cherry tomatoes*
- 6 *ounces grated cheese (your choice)*

Mix the first five ingredients together. Cut the tops of the tomatoes and hollow out. Stuff the tomatoes with the mixture. Sprinkle with grated cheese. Chill and serve on a plate lined with lettuce.

Dan Dickerson—Started his UM broadcast career as a sideline reporter for WWJ. He has been broadcasting in his native state for more than ten years and now is the voice of UM football for WJR.

Second Quarter
Soups, Salads, and Side Dishes

Chicken Almond Pasta Salad

Bo Schembechler (Millie's)

- 4 *cups cooked cubed chicken*
- 2 *medium apples, cured and chopped (2 cups)*
- 8 *ounces bowtie or corkscrew pasta, cooked and drained*
- 1 *8-ounce can pineapple chunks, drained*
- ½ *cup halved seedless grapes*
- ½ *cup sliced celery*
- ¼ *cup thinly sliced green onion*
- ¾ *cup mayonnaise or salad dressing*
- ⅓ *cup low fat plain yogurt*
- 3 *tablespoons lime juice*
- 1 *tablespoon honey*
- 2 *tablespoons grated gingerroot*
- ¼ *teaspoon salt*
- ½ *cup toasted sliced almonds*

In a large bowl toss chicken, apples, pasta, pineapples, grapes, celery, and onion. For dressing, combine mayonnaise, yogurt, lime juice, honey, gingerroot, and salt. Gently toss dressing and pasta mixture. Cover and chill. Add milk to moisten if necessary when serving.

Tangy Broccoli Salad

Bo Schembechler (Millie's)

1 cup Miracle Whip or Light Miracle Whip salad dressing
2 tablespoons sugar
2 tablespoons vinegar
1 medium bunch broccoli, cut into flowerets
4 cups loosely packed fresh spinach leaves
8 ounces bacon, crisply cooked, crumbled
½ cup red onion, cut into strips
¼ cup raisins

Mix dressing, sugar, and vinegar in large bowl. Add remaining ingredients, mix lightly. Refrigerate. Makes 8 servings.

Corn Chowder

Leo Brown

4 cups corn, cut from cob (about 8 large ears), divided
1 tablespoon margarine
2 cups chopped onion
1 cup diced celery
2 ounces diced, lower-salt deli ham
2 cloves garlic, minced
2½ cups peeled, diced baking potatoes (about 1¼ pounds)
2 10½-ounce cans low-sodium chicken broth
¼ cup plus 2 tablespoons all-purpose flour
½ teaspoon salt
¼ teaspoon black pepper
⅛ teaspoon ground red pepper
2 cups 2% milk
1 teaspoon Worcestershire sauce

Position knife blade in food processor bowl; add 2½ cups corn. Process until smooth; set aside.

Melt margarine in a large Dutch oven over medium heat. Add onion and next 3 ingredients, and sauté 10 minutes or until vegetables are tender, stirring occasionally. Add potato and broth; bring to a boil. Reduce heat and simmer, uncovered, 20 minutes or until potato is tender, stirring frequently. Add the corn puree and remaining 1½ cups corn. Cook 10 minutes.

Place flour and next 3 ingredients in a small bowl. Gradually add milk and Worcestershire sauce, blending with a wire whisk; add to chowder. Cook over medium heat 10 minutes or until thickened, stirring constantly.

Hamburger Soup

Roosevelt Smith

3 tablespoons butter
1½ pounds ground chuck
1 28-ounce can tomatoes, drained
2 cans condensed beef consommé
1 can onion soup
4 medium carrots, sliced
1 can corn, drained
¼ cup chopped celery tops
½ cup chopped parsley
1 bay leaf
½ teaspoon dried oregano
¼ teaspoon pepper
½ cup uncooked tiny macaroni
grated Parmesan cheese

Brown beef and drain fat. Add all ingredients except pasta and cheese. Heat to boiling; reduce heat and simmer 30 minutes. Return soup to boil, add pasta. Boil 15-20 minutes more. Sprinkle with grated cheese and serve with French bread.

Roosevelt Smith—This Detroit, Michigan, native was a tailback from 1977 to 1979. He ran for a career total of 866 yards, 157 yards coming in a game against Wisconsin during his sophomore season.

Macaroni and Cheese (the Very Best)

Tripp Welborne

1 8-ounce package macaroni
2 sticks butter
8 ounces longhorn cheese
8 ounces Colby cheese
4 eggs
milk to desired consistency (not much)

Preheat water. Boil macaroni for 10 minutes. While it is boiling, add a pinch of salt. Drain. Add 3 eggs, butter, cheeses, and a little milk. Put in casserole dish.

Heat 1 cup milk to boiling. Break 1 egg over milk, stirring, and heat a couple of seconds. Pour over casserole. Sprinkle some grated cheddar cheese over top. Sprinkle pepper over top. Bake in 350° oven for 10 minutes.

Tripp Welborne—Two-time all-American strong safety who played on three Big Ten championship squads. The four-year letter winner (1987–90) led the Wolverines in interceptions in 1988 and in punt-return yardage in 1989 and 1990.

Kozmo's Coleslaw

Jim Kozlowski

Salad

⅓–½ cup dried blueberries or cherries
⅓ cup chopped green onions
⅓ cup toasted sunflower seeds
3 carrots, chopped
1 16-ounce package coleslaw mix
1 11-ounce can mandarin orange segments (reserve juice)

Dressing

3 tablespoons firmly packed brown sugar
½ teaspoon pepper
¼ teaspoon salt
¼ teaspoon dried basil leaves
3 tablespoons white vinegar
1 tablespoon mandarin orange juice
1 beef-flavored packet from Ramen noodle soup (set noodles aside)
½ cup olive or vegetable oil

Mix together salad. In a separate bowl, stir together dressing ingredients whisk, gradually adding oil. Refrigerate 1 hour. Pour dressing over salad, top with noodles.

Jim Kozlowski—Defensive back for the Woverines from 1976 to 1980. "Koz," as friends still call him, continued his success off the field as a business executive with the soft drink company, Dr. Pepper.

Escalloped Corn

William F. Dufek

1 *17-ounce can whole kernel corn*
1 *17-ounce can creamed corn*
2 *eggs, slightly beaten*
1 *cup sour cream*
½ *cup melted butter*
1 *box Jiffy corn muffin mix*

Mix all ingredients together. Pour into 2-quart casserole dish. Bake at 350° for 1 hour.

William Dufek—A four-year letter winner for Michigan, Dufek was part of three Big Ten Champion teams. A tackle from 1974 to 1978, the Grand Rapids native was an all-Big Ten selection in 1976.

In-House Tailgate Party Cream of Wild Rice Soup

Brian J. Dickey

- 2 *cups cooked wild rice*
- 1 *large onion, diced*
- ½ *green pepper, diced*
- 1½ *ribs celery, diced*
- 2 *large fresh mushrooms or 1 small can*
- ½ *cup butter or 1 stick*
- 1 *cup flour*
- 8 *cups hot chicken broth*
- *salt and pepper*
- 1 *cup light cream or half-and-half*
- 2 *tablespoons dry white Michigan wine*

Prepare the wild rice according to the package; set aside. Sauté the onion, green pepper, celery, and mushrooms in butter about 3 minutes or just until vegetables soften. Sprinkle in the flour, stirring and cooking until flour is mixed in but do not let it begin to brown. Add chicken stock, blend well. Add cooked rice, stir in cream. Add dry white Michigan wine. Heat gently but do not boil. About 12 servings. Serve with ice cold adult beverage, plenty of maize and blue napkins.

B. J. Dickey—A quarterback, he saw action in both the 1979 Gator Bowl and the 1981 Bluebonnet Bowl. Started seven games in 1979 and lettered four times for UM.

Spinach Salad

Paul Girgash

- *1 pound fresh spinach*
- *1 medium onion*
- *8 ounces fresh mushrooms*
- *1 can (11 ounces) mandarin oranges, drained*
- *1 pint strawberries*
- *4 slices bacon, cooked crisp and crumbled*
- *1 bottle sweet and sour dressing*

Wash spinach. Dry, remove stems, and tear up. Slice onion thin and separate into rings. Trim mushroom stems, rinse, and slice. Drain oranges and hull strawberries. In a large container, toss ingredients. Turn into 6-quart salad bowl or two bowls and add dressing, lightly. Sprinkle with bacon and serve. Makes about 18 cups of salad.

Paul Girgash—A 1982 all-Big Ten selection at linebacker, Girgash played four seasons for the maize and blue. He started 36 career games, including the 1981 and 1983 Rose Bowls.

Pasta Salad

M. Kirk Taylor

1 pound spaghetti cooked
½-¾ jar (depending on desired spicy taste) salad seasoning
8 ounces Wishbone Italian dressing (more or less to taste)
2 cups broccoli, chopped
2 cups cauliflower, chopped
1 medium cucumber, chopped
1 small red onion, chopped
2-3 bunches green onion, chopped
2 medium tomatoes, seeded and chopped
½ green pepper, chopped
½ red pepper, chopped
green or black olives to taste

Marinate spaghetti in salad seasoning and Italian dressing refrigerated overnight. Add chopped vegetables in morning and continue to refrigerate and marinate until serving.

Kirk Taylor—A five-time letter winner for Michigan's basketball team, Taylor averaged 4.5 points per game for the 1988–89 National Champions. He finished third on the team, with 10.4 points per game in 1990–91.

Hamburgered Baked Beans

Anthony Carter

1 *16–20-ounce can pork and beans*
1 *pound ground beef*
¼ *onion*
¼ *green pepper*
2 *cups unpacked dark brown sugar*
dab mustard

Preheat oven to 425°. Put can of pork and beans in large oven-type pan; *do not drain juice.* Cook ground beef until done and drain excess fat. Dice onion and green pepper. Combine brown sugar into pork and beans, stirring until sugar dissolves. Add ground beef and stir until evenly distributed. Add diced onion and green pepper and dab of mustard. Stir all ingredients together. Put in oven and cook about 20-25 minutes or until onion and green peppers are soft. Stir occasionally so beans don't stick to sides or bottom of pan.

Caponata

Joe Paterno

2 pounds eggplant, peeled and cut into ½″ cubes (about 8 cups)
salt
½ cup olive oil
2 cups finely chopped celery
¾ cup finely cut onions
⅓ cup wine vinegar mixed with 4 teaspoons sugar
3 cups drained canned Italian plum or whole-pack tomatoes
2 tablespoons tomato sauce
6 large green olives, pitted, slivered, and well rinsed
2 tablespoons capers
4 flat anchovy fillets, well rinsed and pounded into a paste with a mortar and pestle
freshly ground black pepper
2 tablespoons pine nuts

Sprinkle the cubes of eggplant generously with salt and set them in a colander or large sieve over paper towels to drain. After about 30 minutes, pat the cubes dry with fresh paper towels and set them aside.

In a heavy 12″-14″ skillet, heat half of the olive oil. Add the celery and cook over moderate heat, stirring frequently, for 10 minutes. Stir in the onions and cook for another 8 to 10 minutes, or until the celery and onions are soft and lightly colored. With a slotted spoon, transfer them to a bowl. Pour the remaining ¼ cup of olive oil into the skillet and over high heat, sauté the eggplant cubes in it, stirring and turning them constantly for about 8 minutes or until they are lightly browned. Return the celery and onions to the skillet and stir in the vinegar and sugar, drained tomatoes, tomato paste, green olives, capers, anchovies, 2 teaspoons salt, and a few grindings of pepper. Bring to a boil, reduce the heat, and simmer uncovered, stirring frequently, for about 15 minutes. Stir in the pine nuts. Taste the mixture and season it with salt and pepper and a little extra vinegar if necessary. Transfer the caponata to a serving bowl and refrigerate until ready to serve.

Antipasto

Joe Paterno

- 4 *raw carrots*
- 4 *green peppers*
- 2 *large onions*
- 1 *stalk celery*
- 1 *pound fresh mushrooms*
- 1 *cauliflower (fresh)*
- 1 *cup olive oil*
- 2 *small bottles catsup (28 ounces)*
- 3 *teaspoons salt*
- 2 *bottles chili sauce (small)*
- 2 *teaspoons Ac´cent*
- 2 *cloves garlic (optional)*
- *juice of 2 lemons*
- 1 *can tuna (drained)*
- 1 *pound frozen king crab meat, defrosted and drained*
- 2 *jars artichoke hearts, drained*
- ½ *cup pitted green olives*
- ½ *cup ripe olives*

Dice or chop carrots, green peppers, onions, celery, mushrooms, and cauliflower, then cook in olive oil as follows: cook carrots for 5 minutes, add onions, mushrooms, and cauliflower for 2 minutes. Add celery and green peppers and cook for 3 minutes.

Mix catsup, salt, chili sauce, Ac´cent, garlic, and lemon juice in a large bowl. Chop or break up the following into the sauce: tuna, crab meat, artichoke hearts, green and ripe olives. Add the cooked vegetables to the above. Mix everything together and let it marinate in the refrigerator for 24 hours. May be served hot or cold.

Spaghetti Salad

Joelle Lukasiewicz

- *1 pound thin spaghetti noodles*
- *12-16 ounces Italian dressing*
- *1 medium or large green pepper*
- *¾ head broccoli*
- *1 large tomato*
- *Salad Supreme seasoning*

Cook noodles until medium soft. Drain and rinse. In a large bowl mix noodles, chopped-small green pepper, chopped-small broccoli, chopped-small tomatoes. Add Italian dressing (to taste) and ½–¾ jar of Salad Supreme seasoning mix. Toss well. Cover and chill overnight or for 3–4 hours. Serve cold.

Note: to make a fat-free dish, use fat-free Italian dressing.

Joelle Lucasiewicz—This WKBD reporter has spent many a weekend night covering victory celebrations for the maize and blue. She has spent ten years reporting in Michigan and has seen her share of the Wolverines' big wins.

Cold Pasta Salad

Eli Zaret

Dressing

- *⅔ cup olive oil*
- *5 tablespoons red wine vinegar*
- *¼ cup chopped fresh basil leaves (or 2 tablespoons dried)*
- *3 tablespoons grated Parmesan cheese*
- *1 tablespoon fresh oregano (or ½ tablespoon dried)*
- *1 teaspoon salt*
- *½ teaspoon ground black pepper*

Salad

- *1 pound rotelle pasta, cooked, rinsed, and drained*
- *1 red pepper, sliced thin*
- *1½ cups broccoli florets, cooked 2 minutes, rinsed, chilled*
- *½ cup sliced, pitted black olives*
- *1 cup cherry tomatoes, sliced in half*
- *½ cup light mayonnaise (or mayonnaise-based salad dressing)*

Prepare dressing first. In a blender, mix together olive oil, red wine vinegar, basil leaves, cheese, oregano, salt and pepper; set aside.

In a large bowl, combine pasta and vegetables; toss salad with oil and vinegar dressing. Refrigerate 8 hours or overnight. At serving time, toss salad with ½ cup mayonnaise. This is a fabulous summer salad. Light, healthy, and delicious.

Eli Zaret—One of Detroit's favorite voices, he has covered the Wolverines for both WDIV-TV and WJBK-TV.

Risotto à la Milanese

Steve Fisher

5 *tablespoons butter*
1 *small onion, finely chopped*
1 *cup dry white wine*
2 *cups long grain white rice*
1 *teaspoon salt*
¼ *teaspoon white pepper*
½ *teaspoon saffron threads*
5 *cups chicken broth*
3 *tablespoons butter*
1 *cup freshly grated Parmesan cheese*

Melt 5 tablespoons of butter in a 4-quart saucepan over moderate heat. Add onion and stir until transparent but do not brown. Add wine and cook over a brisk flame until evaporated. Add rice, season with salt and white pepper, and stir until every grain is coated with butter. Add saffron and about two cups of chicken broth. Let it almost completely evaporate before adding remaining broth, a little at a time. Reduce heat, continuing to cook, uncovered and stirring frequently, about 20–25 minutes or until it has reached the al dente stage (a nutty-like texture). Remove from heat and add remaining butter plus several tablespoons of the grated cheese. Place rest of cheese in a serving bowl for guests who want extra.

Steve Fisher—Currently the head coach of Michigan's basketball team.

Quick and Easy Baked Beans

Nick Saban

1½ pounds ground chuck
1 large onion, chopped
¼ green pepper, chopped
1 stalk celery, chopped
2 or 3 cans baked beans
¼ cup brown sugar
¼ cup ketchup

In a skillet, brown first four ingredients, drain well, and combine with remaining ingredients in a baking dish. Bake at 350° for 1 hour.

Nick Saban—Saban has been credited with bringing a wealth of success to East Lansing. In just one season at the helm of the Michigan State University football team, he guided MSU to a 6-5-1 mark and a berth to the Independence Bowl—the school's first winning season since 1990.

Tomatoes and Mozzarella with Basil

Kurt Becker

¼ cup olive oil
1½ tablespoons balsamic vinegar
1 tablespoon chopped fresh basil
¾ teaspoon Dijon-style mustard
½ teaspoon salt
⅛ teaspoon pepper
4 medium tomatoes
fresh-sliced mozzarella

Whisk oil, vinegar, basil, mustard, salt, and pepper in a large nonmetal dish. Alternate tomatoes and cheese on a serving plate. Pour mixture over top. Garnish with additional basil leaves. I usually put this in a flat square-shaped Rubbermaid container for tailgating.

Bruschetta of Mozzarella and Sun-Dried Tomato Pesto

Phil Hubbard

- 2 *ounces sun-dried tomatoes*
- 2 *tablespoons fresh basil*
- 4 *cloves garlic*
- ¼ *cup pine nuts, toasted*
- ¼ *cup grated Asiago or Parmesan cheese*
- 2 *teaspoons freshly ground black pepper*
- ¼ *cup olive oil*
- ½ *pound fresh mozzarella*
- 4 *thick slices Italian bread*

Soak tomatoes in warm water to soften. Combine with basil, 2 cloves garlic, pine nuts, Asiago or Parmesan cheese, pepper, and 2 tablespoons olive oil in a food processor and pulse until roughly chopped. Add mozzarella and pulse to blend. Puree remaining olive oil and garlic and brush over bread slices. Lightly toast or grill bread, spread with cheese mixture, and bake in a 350° oven for 5 minutes, or until cheeses have melted. Makes 4 appetizer servings.

Phil Hubbard—A center on the gold medal U.S. Olympic basketball team in 1976, Hubbard played four years for the Wolverines, serving as captain in both 1978 and 1979. The Canton, Ohio, native scored 1,455 points in 88 games for UM before playing in the NBA with the Detroit Pistons and the Cleveland Cavaliers.

Baked Zucchini

Jim Harbaugh

- *6 medium zucchinis*
- *⅓ cup olive or salad oil*
- *1 small onion*
- *½ green pepper, minced*
- *1 clove garlic, chopped*
- *½ teaspoon rosemary*
- *1 tablespoon parsley, chopped*
- *3 eggs*
- *½ cup grated cheese*
- *buttered bread crumbs*

Cook onion, green pepper, garlic, rosemary, and parsley in oil until soft. Cook zucchini in boiling salted water until tender. Mash cooked zucchini and add the oil mixture. Mix with the eggs, well beaten, and grated cheese. Place in a buttered casserole dish, top with bread crumbs, and bake at 350° for 40 minutes.

Onion Soup

James Pickens

6 onions
1 or 2 10¾ ounce cans of beef stock
bread, cubed
mozzarella cheese
¼ cup white wine

Fry onions in wine (to cook sugar out of onions). Cook long. Then add beef stock. Put in oven-safe soup bowls or large casserole dish, top with bread and cheese. Bake at 350° until cheese is melted.

James Pickens—The defensive back was a second-team all-Big Ten selection in 1975 and 1976, moving up to the first team in 1977. Pickens started each of the 36 games of his career over his three seasons as the Wolverines compiled a record of 28-6-2.

Cranberry Salad

Derrick Walker

1 package (large) red Jell-O
1½ cups boiling water
1 can cranberry sauce
1 cup sour cream

Dissolve Jell-O in hot water; chill until slightly thick.

Beat cranberry sauce and sour cream until smooth; mix in Jell-O mixture. Chill 8 hours.

Derrick Walker—Walker was named a first-team all-Big Ten selection at tight end in 1989 when he caught 12 passes for 110 yards. The Glenwood, Illinois, native started all twelve games his senior year, and played in two Rose Bowls.

German Potato Salad

Elvis Grbac

8 slices smoked bacon
1 cup onions
2½ tablespoons flour
2½ tablespoons sugar
2½ tablespoons salt
1 teaspoon celery seed
dash pepper
1 cup water
less than ½ cup vinegar
3½–4 pounds potatoes, red or white

Crisp bacon and cook onion in bacon drippings. Stir in seasonings until bubbles appear. Remove and add water and vinegar. Return crushed bacon; stir and heat. Boil 1 minute. Quarter potatoes and cook. Cut into quarter-inch slices while warm. Add warm sauce.

After cooking bacon, drain off most of the fat and add oil or water if needed to cook onions. Vinegar and sugar can be adjusted to taste. Prepare sauce early and allow to set to marinate together. Serve warm for best flavor.

Elvis Grbac—As a quarterback, Grbac lead the Wolverines to victory in the 1991 Gator Bowl and the 1993 Rose Bowl. Before being drafted by the San Francisco 49ers, Grbac set six career records, including the most passing yards (6,460).

Cheesy Ham and Rice

Dan Dierdorf

½ cup green peppers, diced
½ cup celery, diced
½ cup onion, diced
2 tablespoons butter
2 tablespoons flour
2 cups evaporated milk
1½ cups grated sharp cheddar cheese
2 cups ham, cooked and julienned
1 teaspoon dry mustard
1 teaspoon garlic salt
¼ teaspoon red pepper
1 teaspoon Worcestershire sauce
3 cups cooked rice

Sauté green pepper, celery, and onion in butter over low heat until tender. Blend in flour. Add milk and cook until sauce is thick and smooth, stirring constantly. Add cheese and heat until melted, stirring constantly again. Add ham, mustard, salt, Worcestershire, and red pepper. Spoon over cooked rice.

Cheesy Potatoes

Steve Garagiola

2 *pounds frozen hashed browns(thaw overnight in refrigerator)*
1 *cup diced onions*
1 *pound carton of sour cream*
8 *ounces grated sharp cheddar cheese*
1 *cup crushed Ruffles potato chips*
1 *10¾-ounce can cream of chicken soup*
1 *stick (¼ pound) margarine, melted*
salt and pepper to taste

Mix all ingredients except potato chips. Pour into a 9″ x 13″ baking dish and top with crumbled chips. Bake 1 hour at 375°.

Don't worry about leftovers; you won't have any.

Wolverine Salad

Ron Kramer

tomato (beefsteak, if in season, preferred)
onion(Vidalia, if in season, preferred)
fresh pineapple

Cut tomato, onion, and pineapple into ¼-½ inch slices; layer. Use your preferred dressing and enjoy the great taste of this combination. Salt, pepper, and spice to your liking.

True Blue Lobster Stew

Roger Bettis

- *1 lobster tail*
- *4 medium potatoes, diced*
- *3 stalks celery, diced*
- *2 carrots, diced*
- *2 medium sweet onions, diced*
- *½ stick butter*
- *3 slices bacon*
- *2 teaspoons Worcestershire sauce*
- *½ cup white wine*
- *1 14-ounce can College Inn chicken broth*
- *½ pint heavy cream*
- *2 envelopes white sauce (such as Knorr Classic Sauces)*
- *3 envelopes cream of vegetable soup, thicken with cornstarch if desired*
- *garlic salt, onion salt (or powder), pepper to taste*

Place lobster tail in a medium kettle with an optional package Stouffer's Lobster Newburg. Add potatoes, celery, carrots, sweet onions and simmer with butter and bacon until tender. Add Worcestershire sauce, white wine, College Inn chicken broth, heavy cream, white sauce, cream of vegetable soup. Add onion salt (or powder), garlic salt, and pepper to taste. Cook on low or medium low until thick.

Roger Bettis—Quarterback on Michigan's 1977 Big Ten Champion team, the Minerva, Ohio, native passed for 114 yards with the varsity reserves in 1975.

Green Bean and Mozzarella Salad

Neal Morton

- *2 cups fresh green beans, cooked and drained*
- *8 ounce mozzarella cheese cut into ½" cubes*
- *½ cup prepared Good Seasons zesty Italian salad dressing*
- *6 fresh plum tomatoes, sliced*
- *⅓ cup chopped fresh basil*
- *⅛ teaspoon pepper*

Mix all ingredients in a large bowl. Cover; refrigerate 1 hour.

Neal Morton—A walk-on to Michigan's basketball team, Morton earned a scholarship for the 1995–96 season. He played in 26 games for Michigan during his senior year.

P-Formation Salad

George Lilja

- *2 16-ounce packages frozen peas (leave frozen; they'll thaw in salad during drive to game)*
- *1 pound bacon, fried, drained, and crumbled (cut uncooked bacon into small pieces first, then cook in tall saucepan and drain—much less mess)*
- *½ cup chopped celery*
- *½ cup chopped green onion*
- *2 teaspoons sugar*
- *1 teaspoon salt*
- *1 teaspoon pepper*
- *1 cup mayonnaise*
- *8 ounces chopped cashews*
- *½ cup shredded cheddar cheese*
- *1 head lettuce*

Wash and drain lettuce. Combine mayonnaise, bacon, peas, salt, pepper, onion, sugar, cashews and celery. In a large bowl, toss together lettuce and mayonnaise mixture, sprinkle with cheese.

George Lilja—The cocaptain of the 1980 team, Lilja was named an all-American during his senior year. A member of three Big Ten Champion teams, the center embarked on a six-year NFL career after his collegiate days were over.

Wild Rice Seafood Casserole

William Dufek

1 ¼ cups Uncle Ben's Long Grain and Wild rice
1 green pepper
1 cup celery
1 Bermuda onion, sliced
1 pound mushrooms sliced and sautéed
1 ½ pounds shrimp
1 teaspoon curry powder
1 teaspoon Worcestershire sauce
1 ½ cups mayonnaise
salt and pepper to taste

Cook rice according to directions on the box. Mix all ingredients lightly in a greased casserole. Bake 45 minutes at 350°. Buttered bread crumbs may be sprinkled over the top. Serves 8.

Blow Out the Buckeyes Baked Beans

Diane Dietz

5 large cans Campbell's pork and beans, drained
2½ pounds ground round
3 medium onions
1 cup brown sugar
1 cup Heinz ketchup
1 cup seafood cocktail sauce
4 tablespoons prepared (dry) mustard
4 tablespoons Worcestershire sauce
1 pound bacon (remove fat)

Brown ground round and onions; strain well. Mix together beans, brown sugar, ketchup, seafood cocktail sauce, dry mustard, and Worcestershire sauce. Place 2" strips of bacon next to each other on top. Bake at 350° until bacon is done (about 1½ hours).

Diane Dietz aka Double D—Former UM women's basketball player. She is a four-time letter winner for the Wolverines. She is still the all-time leading scorer with 2,066 points. Diane is also an Academic all-American and the winner of the Gerald R. Ford Award. She was elected to Michigan's Hall of Fame in 1996.

Fred's Favorite Pasta

Fred McLeod

- 2 *tablespoons olive oil*
- 1 *clove garlic, minced*
- 1 *tablespoon basil*
- 2 *tablespoons parsley*
- 1 *28-ounce can whole, peeled tomatoes with juice*
- 6 *ounces mozzarella, cubed*
- 1 *pound rigatoni noodles, cooked*

Sauté minced garlic, careful not to let the garlic brown. Add basil and parsley; stir. Cook over medium heat for 1 minute. Add the juice from the tomatoes. Cut the tomatoes into bite-size pieces. Stir tomatoes into the sauce mixture. Let simmer for ten minutes over low heat. While the sauce is simmering cook the pasta according to the directions on the box. Drain pasta, toss with sauce. Mix well. Just before serving, add the cubed cheese. Stir quickly, because the cheese melts fast. Serve immediately.

Fred McLeod—The WDIV-TV sportscaster is the voice of Piston Basketball on PASS sports. He loves that game, but professes a love of the UM football program. The Pittsburgh native is also known in sports circles as a stellar baseball player. When he is not working weekends, Fred sneaks out to a few Wolverine games to get his weekly fix.

Low-Fat Chicken Pasta Salad
Mitch Albom

- *1 14-ounce box Mueller's salad macaroni*
- *6 boneless, skinless chicken breasts (cooked, cooled, and cubed)*
- *1 medium cucumber (peeled, cored, and cubed in tiny pieces)*
- *8 ounces light Italian dressing (or, for less fat, half light and half fat free)*
- *1 medium tomato (cut in tiny pieces)*
- *2 tablespoons McCormick salad seasonings*
- *8 cherry tomatoes (sliced to put on top of salad)*

Toss everything together and put in a bowl. If prepared the night before, wait to put cherry tomato slices on the top, as the salad soaks up the dressing and you may want to add a little more and toss, then put the tomatoes on the top. A side bowl of Parmesan cheese is nice for those who like it on their individual servings.

Mitch Albom—Best known as an award-winning journalist for the Detroit Free Press, *Mitch is also the drive-time host for WJR, a best-selling author and an accomplished musician.*

Ambrosia Fruit Salad

John Wangler (Mama Wang's)

1 package miniature marshmallows
1 large can (about 30 ounces) fruit cocktail
1 can pineapple tidbits or chunks
1 small can mandarin oranges
1 pint fresh whipping cream
1 cup finely chopped nuts (walnuts or pecans)
If in season, fresh peaches or nectarines can be added.

Thoroughly drain all canned fruit. Mix fruit, marshmallows, and nuts until well blended. Whip the cream and fold into the fruit mixture. Chill overnight in the refrigerator.

Halftime Entertainment

Schembechler photo

Besides Millie's good cooking, her smile along with a dash of kindness were always welcome at UM events.

Kalmbach photo

Let the tailgating begin!

UM fans don't have the luxury of great big lots for their tailgates. Their parking is wedged between buildings, practice fields, patches of trees, and fairways of the golf course. But fans use this little setback to their advantage. With the tailgating tables set with candelabras and cloth napkins, who can resist the temptation to try a sample of your neighbor's home cooking?

Look around! Maize and blue flags are the backdrop for every scene. "Hail to the Victors" plays from every car radio. And the air is filled with smells of chili, burgers, brats, plenty of beer, mixed drinks, pop, and corn chips. The chips, a blue-blooded UM tailgate favorite, have to be

Kalmbach photo

maize and blue. That's right—if there is a way to serve blue and gold food, UM fans will do it!

Just before the game, the UM band marches through the parking area to the stadium. Fans get pumped up with the sound of the drums and cymbals and the cheers of "Go Blue!" The tailgaters know when they hear the band it's time to pack up and head into the stadium.

Let's Hear it for the Band

Wondering how this tradition began at the University of Michigan? Well, then look no further than the students in Ann Arbor. In 1896 a few musically inspired students decided to put some music to the events happening around school. According to the trivia buffs who hang out in the UM library, the first band rehearsal took place in Harris Hall. In 1897, the band thought they sounded pretty good, so too did then-president of the University James Burrill Angell And so the band took their show on the road. Their first public appearance was at old University Hall during the law school's annual observance of Washington's birthday. The first time the maize and blue band took to the football field was in the fall of 1989.

Dattilo photo

Into the Stadium

Leading the way...
The UM marching band leads tailgaters into the largest college-owned structure of its kind. The Stadium was designed solely for football and hails ninety rows closer to the playing field with no running back, no posts, or other obstructions. Capacity: 101,701

Running the yards...
The Stadium was completed in 1927 at a cost of more than $950,000. It initially held 72,000 spectators, but was increased to 84,401 by the addition of temporary wooden bleachers. In 1949, permanent steel stands replaced the wooden bleachers, increasing the capacity to 97,239. Football fever grew in Michigan and seating capacity had to be increased to 101,001 in 1956 and to 101,701 in 1973.

Touchdown!
The first UM football game was played October 1, 1927. Michigan, led by captain Bennie Oosterbaan, defeated Ohio Wesleyan, 33-0. Laverne (Kip) Taylor, Michigan end, scored the first touchdown in the stadium on a 28-yard pass from halfback Louis Gilbert.

Score!
The dedication game was played on October 22, 1927. Michigan defeated Ohio State, 21-0. And the rivalry began...

Dattilo photo

Go Blue!

Since the opening of the stadium in 1927, more than 30 million fans have watched the Wolverines play over 400 games. Highlights include November 20, 1993, when stadium and NCAA attendance were at a record high with fans totaling 106,867. Ohio State always brings out the best in us! Also set in 1993, NCAA season record of 739,560.

Bo's Best

According to Bo there are three great quarters he will always remember and one quarter he would like to forget. As in typical Bo fashion, let's start with his best.

Kalmbach photo

October 23, 1982 at Evanston, Illinois

Second Quarter

In the tough Big Ten, it's not often that a college football team scores 35 points in a single game. On a sunny October day in Evanston, Bo's boys did it in one single quarter. Michigan had grabbed a 7-0 lead after the first period, but was in the midst of a 73-yard drive when the first-quarter gun sounded.

Steve Smith took the ball in for a touchdown from 11 yards out to open the second quarter and the Wolverines were off and running. After Northwestern went three plays and out, Michigan drove 76 yards for a touchdown as Smith ran for a one-yard score. The Wildcats were forced to punt after three plays again, and Smith capped a 76-yard drive with a 34-yard scoring pass to Anthony Carter. Northwestern just couldn't cut it on its next possession and Smith and Carter connected again—this time for 29 yards and Michigan's fourth touchdown of the quarter.

After Northwestern fumbled the kickoff, it took just two plays for Smith to find Dunaway in the end zone, and Michigan scored its 5th, yes, 5th touchdown of the period. The thirty-five points in a quarter set a Michigan standard for points in a period. What a period!

Hail to the Victors

In the 1890s, the winner of the annual Thanksgiving Day battle between Michigan and Chicago could claim the title "Best in the West." When Michigan won the big game in 1898, after two years of humiliating defeat, overjoyed UM students paraded to the Chicago campus as the marching band played "Hot Time in the Old Town Tonight."

One of those students was Louis Elbel. As he later recalled, "It struck me quite suddenly that such an epic should be dignified by something more elevating, for it was no ordinary victory. My spirits were so uplifted that I was clear off the earth and that is when 'The Victors' was inspired."

Elbel thought the Michigan spirit needed "a fitting paean, a clarion call, something simple but grand and heroic." Elbel composed that fitting piece of music, but knew that a band was necessary to "bring out the proper vim." A short time later, an arrangement was produced for a full band. By chance, John Philip Sousa was appearing in Ann Arbor and Elbel boldly offered his composition. Sousa agreed to include it in the evening's performance and "The Victors" had its public debut on April 19, 1899 at University Hall. (Based on an article by Louis Elbel in *Michigan Chimes*, January 1922)

"The Victors"

Hail! To the victors valiant
Hail! To the conquering heroes,
Hail! Hail! To Michigan, the leaders and best
Hail! To the victors valiant
Hail! To the conquering heroes,
Hail! Hail! To Michigan, the champions of the west.

Kalmbach photo

The UM Marching Band in a rousing half-time performance.

Fritz Crisler

Coaches of the Year

Fritz Crisler led his 1947 team to a conference title, a Rose Bowl victory, an undefeated season, a number one national ranking, and was named national coach of the year. On that note he retired from coaching.

UM photo

Bennie Oosterbaan

The following year, Bennie Oosterbaan led his squad to a conference title, an undefeated season, and a number one ranking. He too was named coach of the year, the only time different coaches at the same school have been named coach of the year in successive seasons.

First Professional Player

Eddie Usher, who played in the backfield and at end for Michigan in 1918 and 1920–21, was the first Wolverine to go on to a professional football career. He signed with the Buffalo All-Americans in 1921 and then played for the Rock Island Independents, Green Bay Packers, and Detroit Lions before retiring in 1925. A total of 209 Wolverines have gone on to play professional football (as of 1995).

Here are a few of the contributors who went on to the pros. Don't forget to look for their recipes.

Indianapolis Colts photo

Jim Harbaugh

UM photo

Anthony Carter

UM photo

Tripp Welborne

UM photo

Ron Kramer

UM photo

Jerret Irons

UM photo

Elvis Grbac

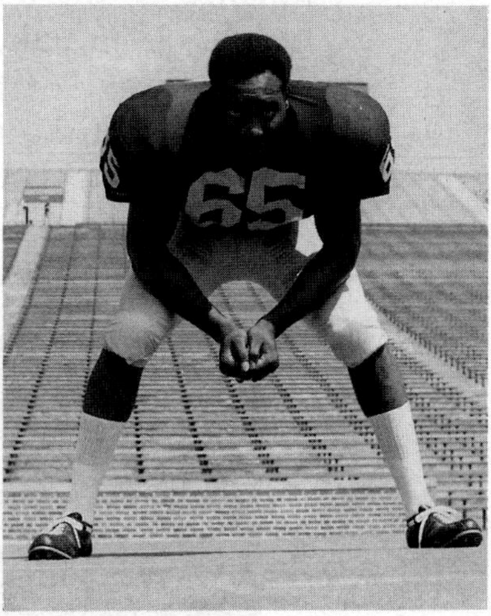
UM photo

Reggie McKenzie

UM photo

Bubba Paris

Heisman Trophy

The Heisman Trophy has been given to the outstanding college football player each year since 1935. Michigan has had two winners: Tom Harmon in 1940 and Desmond Howard in 1991. Nineteen Wolverines have finished in the top ten in the Heisman voting. Harmon, 1939, and Bob Chappuis, 1947, have placed second. Three have finished in the third spot: Rob Lyric, 1976, Rick Leach, 1978, and Jim Harbaugh, 1906. Bob Timberlake, 1964, and Anthony Carter, 1982, have finished fourth in the voting. Carter finished among the top ten voters his sophomore, junior, and senior seasons, and Ron Kramer joins Leach and Harmon as two-time top ten finishers.

Bynum photo

Desmond Howard posing here with his Heisman. He went on to win the Super Bowl MVP, only the fourth man in history to win both.

Kalmbach photo

Oldest Records

Records are made to be broken, but a few Michigan football records have stood for a long time. Willie Heston, 1901–4, scored 72 touchdowns in his career, 18 more than runner-up Tyrone Wheatley. In 1902 Al Herrnstein set the season TD record with 26 and a single-game record of 7 against Michigan Agricultural College (now MSU). James E. Duffy's 55-yard field goal against Cornell in 1891 stood as the Michigan best for 97 years before Mike Gillette bettered it by one yard in 1988.

Another of Bo's Best

January 1, 1986 at Tempe Arizona--3rd quarter

At the Fiesta Bowl, Michigan's desire to reach the 10-win mark looked pretty dismal. Nebraska came out smoking and grabbed a 14-3 halftime lead. The Huskers took the kick-off to start in the second half, but fumbled the ball away after three plays.

Michigan took advantage of this opportunity. The boys closed the gap to 14-10 when Gerald White ran for a one-yard touchdown. The Wolverine defense forced Nebraska to cough up the ball on its next possession. From the 38-yard line, quarterback Jim Harbaugh rallied the troops down to the one-yard line! Nebraska gained just one first down in its next drive, and David Arnold broke through the line and blocked the first punt attempt. Pat Moons kicked a 19-yard field goal four plays later for a 10-14 Michigan lead!

The quarter continued to go the Wolverine's way. Nebraska was forced to punt after just three plays. Then Michigan used a 7-play, 52-yard drive to score on Harbaugh's two-yard carry. The 24 point quarter enabled Michigan to bring home a 27-23 win.

Way to go 10-win mark!

The Little Brown Jug

The Little Brown Jug that goes to the winner of the Minnesota-Michigan game is one of the most famous trophies in college football. It is also surrounded by myths. In fact, the original jug wasn't brown, it wasn't very little, it wasn't carried from Ann Arbor to Minnesota for the 1903 game, and it wasn't "captured" by Minnesota janitor Oscar Munson.

UM trainer Keene Fitzpatrick had suspicions that Minnesota might doctor the water provided on the sidelines. Student manager Tommy Roberts was sent to a Minneapolis variety store where he bought a cream-colored, five-gallon jug for 30 cents. With two minutes left in the game, Minnesota scored a touchdown to tie the game at 6-6.

The Minnesota crowd swarmed onto the field and the last two minutes were never played, ending Michigan's three-year winning streak. Roberts was swept up in the crowd and simply abandoned his jug. Munson found it the next day in the litter of the stadium and took it to the athletic director, who had it labeled "Michigan's Jug Captured by Oscar, October 31, 1903."

When the two teams next played, in 1909, Minnesota sent a message: "We have your Little Brown Jug. Come up and win it." The phrase "brown jug" may have come from a popular song of the day. (Based on an article by Thomas Roberts in the Michigan football program of October 8, 1968.)

UM photo

Earliest Game Film

The earliest film record of Michigan football is that of the 1904 University of Chicago game played in Ann Arbor. The movie, about eight minutes long, was filmed by Edison's American Kinetograph Company. It shows the powerful ground game and bone-jarring line play of Fielding Yost's "point a minute" team. The *Michigan Daily* quoted the cameraman as saying he had captured "excellent pictures of your great Heston, mountainous Carter and Curtis, and I secured close-up pictures of the men who were jounced into slumberland."

The Wings Have It…

Michigan's famed winged helmet dates way back—back to 1938, when Fritz Crisler, a man with an eye for detail and cool colors, arrived from Princeton.

Fritz says he remembers those days back when and decided Michigan had to do something to dress up that boring black helmet. And so the football program added a little corn color—you know, maize—and the Wolverine blue. And then he decided to use the same basic helmet those football guys at Princeton were using.

Fritz says his best idea was the wing on the helmet. He thought the quarterbacks would be able to see the receivers better if they stood out in the crowd. Sure enough 60 years later the Wolverines are a standout, and I am sure the helmets helped.

UM photo

President Gerald Ford in his playing days.

Retired Numbers

Five Michigan numbers have been retired in honor of seven players, six of them linemen, and all of them two-way players. Tom Harmon's "old 98" was the first, followed by Ben Oosterbaan's number, 47. Brothers Francis, Albert, and Alvin Wistert all played, all were named all-American, and all wore number 11. Ron Kramer's number, 87, will forever symbolize rugged play at defensive end and spectacular catches on offense. Number 48, worn by Gerald Ford, was officially retired during halftime of the 1994 game against Michigan State. Ford's gridiron stats may not quite match those of fellow Michigan stars, but he did make his mark in other fields.

Radio

The first UM football game broadcast was in 1924. Ty Tyson lugged a portable transmitter into the Ferry Field stands for the Wisconsin contest. Fielding Yost permitted the broadcast over WWJ only after assuring the game was sold out and even then made Tyson pay for his seat .

The true voice of the maize and blue, however, was Bob Ufer. He broadcast 362 consecutive games over 37 year, and there was never any doubt that he was a "Meechigan" partisan. Only Ufer could use the analogy "running like a penguin, with a hot herring in his cummerbund" to describe Anthony Carter's game-winning, last-second touchdown against Indiana in 1979.

"The Yellow and the Blue"

Sing to the colors that float in the night
Hurrah for the yellow and blue!
Yellow the stars as they ride through the night
And reel in a rollicking crew.
Yellow the field where ripens the grain
And yellow the moon on the harvest wain—
Hail!
Hail to the colors that float in the light
Hurrah for the yellow and blue!

Blue are the billows that bow to the sun
When yellow-robed morning is due.
Blue are the curtains that evening has spun
The slumbers of Phoebus to woo.
Blue are the blossoms to memory dear
And blue is the sapphire and gleams like a tear—
Hail!
Hail to the ribbons that nature has spun
Hurrah for the yellow and blue!
Hail to the college whose colors we wear
Here's to the hearts that are true!
Here's to the maid of the golden hair
And eyes that are brimming with blue!
Garlands of blue bells and maize intertwine
And hearts that are true and voices combine—
Hail!
Hail to the college whose colors we wear:
Hurrah for the yellow and blue!

UM photo

Do You Remember...

Here are a few of the contributors in their playing days.

UM photo

Pete Elliot

Wangler photo

Phil Hubbard

UM photo

Check out their "slam dunk" recipes.

Chris Webber

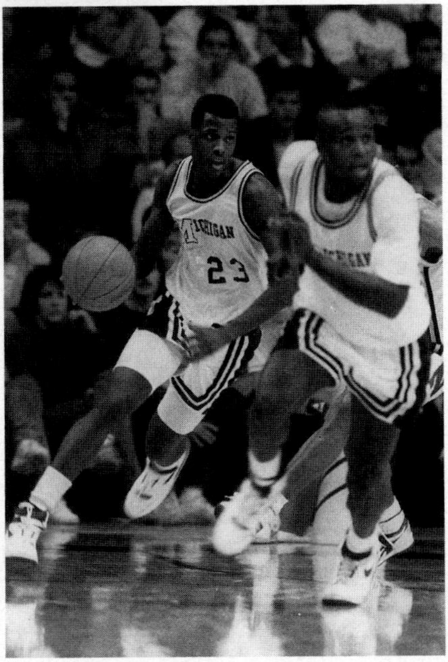

UM photo

Kirk Taylor

UM photo

Rick Leach

These guys have passed along some great techniques.

UM photo

Mike Griffin

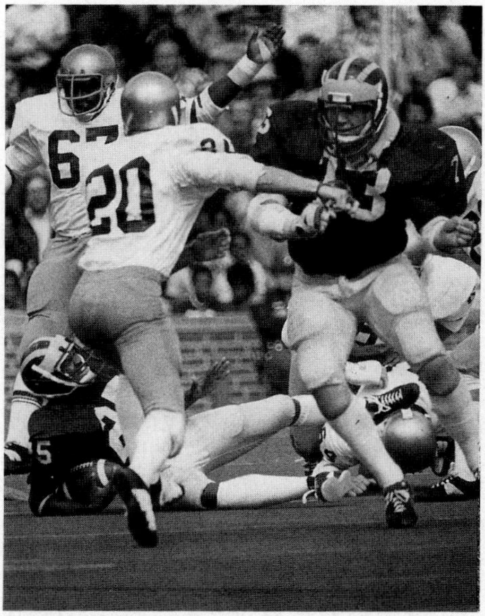

UM photo

William Dufek

Dan Heikkenen

UM photo

Wangler photo

John Wangler

One More of Bo's Best

4th Quarter
September 23, 1978 at South Bend, Indiana

Michigan and Notre Dame renewed their rivalry for the first time in 35 years and through three quarters had played to a 14-14 tie. Michigan had gained momentum when Curtis Greer recovered a fumble on its own 28-yard line and the Wolverines drove for the tying score.

The Wolverines started the final period with the ball on the Notre Dame 21-yard line, the great field position gained on a Jerry Meter interception. In the new quarter, it took just one play to score, as Rick Leach found Jerry Marsh in the end zone for a 20-14 UM lead.

The Irish never threatened again, as both Notre Dame drives that went more than five plays ended on turnovers. Meanwhile the Wolverines plowed in for another touchdown and added a safety in the final two minutes to take a 28-14 win back from South Bend. Now how's that for a great story to start off your tailgate party.

4th Quarter Comebacks

Games from 1969 to 1989 (the Bo years) in which Michigan has scored in the fourth quarter to break a tie or come back from a deficit to win or tie.

Opponent	Play	Time Left	Final Score
1988			
UCLA	J.D. Carlson 24-yard field goal	0:01	24-23
Ohio State	Demetrius Brown-John Kolesar 41-yard pass	1:32	34-31
Alabama	Demetrius Brown-John Kolesar 20-yard pass	0:50	28-24
1987			
Illinois	Phil Webb 2-yard run	0:43	17-14
1986			
Hawaii	Bob Perryman 2-yard run	14:17	27-10
Iowa	Mike Gilette 34-yard field goal	0:00	20-17
1983			
Washington St	David Hall 4-yard run	6:10	20-17
Iowa	Bob Bergeron 45-yard field goal	0:08	16-13
1981			
Purdue	Steve Smith 26-yard run	11:30	28-10
1980			
Northwestern	Rich Hewlett-Anthony Carter 23-yard pass	10:59	17-10

<u>1979</u>			
Indiana	John Wangler-Anthony Carter 45-yard pass	0:00	27-21
<u>1978</u>			
Arizona	Russell Davis 1-yard run	5:25	21-17
Notre Dame	Rick Leach-Doug Marsh 17-yard pass	14:55	28-14
<u>1975</u>			
Stanford	Bob Wood 42-yard field goal	1:36	19-19
Baylor	Gordon Bell 1-yard run	8:10	14-14
MSU	Gordon Bell 19-yard run	12:09	16-6
Minnesota	Gordon Bell 23-yard run	6:56	28-21
<u>1973</u>			
Ohio State	Dennis Franklin 10-yard run	10:02	10-10
<u>1972</u>			
Purdue	Mike Lantry 30-yard field goal	1:00	9-6
Indiana	Dennis Franklin 12-yard run	9:35	21-7
<u>1971</u>			
Purdue	Dana Coin 25-yard field goal	0:26	20-17
Ohio State	Bill Taylor 21-yard run	2:07	10-7
<u>1970</u>			
Texas A&M	Don Moorhead 7-yard run	3:00	14-10

And now, for the quarter that made everyone lose their appetites.

September 17, 1988 at Ann Arbor, Michigan

It was just four years earlier, in 1984 that Michigan crushed the number one ranked Hurricanes at Michigan stadium. Now, I guess, it was just time for a little sunny Florida revenge. At first, it looked like history would repeat itself. There was sunshine. It was hot, all of the elements from the 1984 game. The Wolverines were even beating Miami 23-14 after three quarters.

By the time the Wolverines got into the fourth quarter, that lead expanded to 30-14. That's when Michael Taylor connected with Chris Calloway on a 16-yard scoring pass. Michigan held this edge midway through the quarter—and then everything fell apart.

Miami quarterback Steve Walsh used 11 consecutive passes to get within 30-22 with 5:40 remaining, then four more passes to score another touchdown. Down 30-28, the Hurricanes tried the onside kick and were successful. They recovered the ball on Michigan's 47-yard line. Seven plays later, Carlos Hueta kicked a 29-yard field goal to give Miami a choking 31-30 win.

Let them eat cake!

"Varsity"

Men of Michigan, on to victory,
Every man in every play—
Michigan expects her varsity to win today.
Rah! rah! rah! rah!
Win for Michigan.

Varsity, down the field,
Never yield, raise high our shield. March on to
victory for Michigan
And the maize and blue—oh, varsity we're for
you,
Here for you, to cheer for you,
We have no fear for you.
Oh, varsity.

Bo Schembechler coached the University of Michigan football team from 1969 to 1989.

Third Quarter
Main Dishes

Cold Marinaded Brisket

Bo Schembechler (Millie's)

1 10½-ounce can consommé
¾ cup soy sauce
¼ cup lemon juice
1-2 teaspoons minced garlic to taste
1 tablespoon liquid smoke
½ cup barbecue sauce
4-5 pounds brisket

Combine ingredients and marinate beef overnight in large plastic container. Cook in preheated 300° oven about an hour per pound. Do not overcook. Cool and slice thin across grain. Can be done 1-2 days ahead. Serve with assorted bread. I use mayonnaise and mustard mixed with horseradish to spread on breads. We used this a lot for sandwiches at tailgates.

Millie's Chicken Dumplings

Bo Schembechler (Millie's)

1 medium roasting hen, trimmed and rinsed (cheescloth optional)
2 14-ounce cans chicken broth
1 large white onion, chopped
3 large stalks celery (with leaves), chopped
½ teaspoon celery salt
2 cups self-rising flour
2 teaspoons chicken seasoning
2 eggs
water

In a large pot, bring to a boil the chicken (tied up in cheesecloth), broth, onion, celery, and celery salt. (Add enough water to cover the chicken 1 inch or so.) Cover and reduce heat to simmer until the chicken is fully cooked and falling off the bone. Remove chicken from broth to a large plate, allow to cool. Keep the remaining broth on warm heat and prepare the dumplings.

Combine the self-rising flour (do not substitute all-purpose baking flour) with the seasoning, eggs, and enough water to make a ball of dough. You will need to add a little flour and water until you get the right consistency to roll out the dough.

Cut dough ball in half and, using a floured surface, roll the dough into a rectangle shape about a ¼ inch thick or less. Using a pizza cutter or knife, cut the rolled-out dough into 1½- to 2-inch squares. Sprinkle the dough with flour so the squares do not stick together. Set aside squares and roll out and cut the rest of the dough. Bring the broth to a boil. (You will need a good amount of broth, about 5 inches deep, to cook the dumplings; add more canned broth at this point if necessary.) One by one, put the squares into the boiling broth, adding them to where the bubbles are coming up. Reduce to warm heat. Bone the cooled chicken, add to the dumplings and stir. Salt and pepper to taste. Makes six large servings.

Millie served this dish with warm dinner rolls and a garden salad. Enjoy!

First and Ten Chili

John Wangler (Mama Wang's)

3 tablespoons cooking oil or bacon grease
3 pounds coarse-ground beef
3 medium onions, finely diced
1 large green pepper, finely diced
1 red bell pepper, finely diced
3 stalks of celery, finely diced
1 tablespoon garlic powder
3 tablespoons chili powder
1 tablespoon cumin
2 tablespoon salt
1 teaspoon cayenne pepper (optional)
3 cans dark red kidney beans, undrained
2 cans great northern beans
1 large can stewed tomatoes (about 30 ounces)

Brown the meat in the hot oil or grease. Add onions, peppers, and celery. Cook on medium heat until slightly soft. Drain grease from pan and add seasonings. Add undrained beans and stewed tomatoes. Cook covered over low heat for 45 minutes, stir mixture frequently. Cook uncovered for 30 minutes to thicken.

Note: make this chili the night before so the flavor is well permeated. Serve over cooked white rice and top with finely chopped green onions and grated cheese or top with small oyster crackers. Enjoy!

Sausage Kramervaro

Ron Kramer

- 2 *pounds Italian sausage (sweet or hot)*
- 1 *large green pepper*
- 1 *large sweet onion*
- *mushrooms (all types)*
- 1 *large red pepper*
- 2 *cups dry red wine*
- *chopped garlic*

Cut sausage to bite size and cook in olive oil for 10 minutes or until brown. Cut vegetables to bite size. Combine sausage and vegetables in a large pot with cover. Add chopped garlic. When mixed, add salt, pepper, and spices to your liking. Before placing in oven, add 2 cups dry red wine. Place in oven at 325° for 1¼ hours. Serve hot. Don't forget Italian bread to dunk in juices from this combination.

Meatball Sandwich

Gaspare Calandrino

2 pounds ground beef
7 ounces bread crumbs
½ tablespoon pepper
½ cup Parmesan cheese
1½ tablespoons chopped parsley
6 large eggs
¼–½ cup water
1½ tablespoons salt
1½ small to medium onions, chopped
1 teaspoon sugar
4–5 large cloves of garlic, finely chopped to taste

Mix ingredients and roll into balls slightly larger than golf balls. Brown meatballs in oil and place in tomato sauce. Cook in sauce for 30 minutes medium heat or 1 hour on simmer. Let cool and cut balls in half. You can freeze meatballs and sauce until game day. Heat at tailgate and serve on small sub bun. Cover with tomato sauce and sprinkle with cheese (Parmesan or mozzarella). Makes about 50 meatballs.

Sauce

2 cloves of chopped garlic
½ onion
8 ounces tomato paste
2 cans tomato juice
1 can water
1 tablespoon sugar
½ tablespoon pepper
1 teaspoon parsley

1 teaspoon sweet basil
1 teaspoon oregano
2 bay leaves

Optional
mushrooms
Italian sausage
wine
more or less garlic, pepper, and spices

Fry garlic and onion in oil until oil turns golden. Fry tomato paste. Add tomato juice and water. Add remaining ingredients.

Gaspare Calandrino—Defensive back on Michigan's 1978 Big Ten Champion football team.

Marinated Steak

Max Richardson

- 3 *pounds T-bone steak*
- 1 *cup oil*
- ¼ *cup wine vinegar*
- 4 *sprigs parsley, chopped*
- 2 *cloves garlic, minced*
- ¼ *teaspoon oregano*
- ¼ *teaspoon pepper*
- *mushrooms and onions*

Place steak in shallow baking dish. Mix oil, vinegar, parsley, garlic, oregano, and pepper and pour over steak. Marinade steak for at least 3 or 4 hours, turning often. Remove steak and pat dry with paper towels. Grill or broil to your own taste. Cover steak with mushrooms and onions and serve.

Mushrooms and Onions

- 1 *pound fresh mushrooms*
- ¼ *cup oil*
- 2 *onions, chopped*
- *salt and pepper to taste*

Sauté mushrooms in oil; add onions and simmer slowly until onions are transparent. Add salt and pepper.

Max Richardson—A four-year letter winner on Michigan's football team from 1974 to 1977, Richardson was a part of three Big Ten title teams. Originally from Fort Wayne, Indiana, Richardson played both wingback and flanker at UM.

A-Maize-ing Beef

Roger Bettis

- *1 2-pound top roast*
- *salt and pepper*
- *garlic powder*
- *3 stalks celery, chopped*

Sprinkle roast with garlic powder, salt, and pepper. Place celery around roast. Wrap in foil. Place in Dutch oven or roaster. Fill with as much water as possible. Cover. Cook at 350° until water boils. Cut back temperature to 275°. Cook 1½ hours. Turn over roast. Cook 1½ hours more until 130° in middle of roast. Slice paper thin.

Creole Gumbo

Jerrett Irons

1 package shrimp-and-crab-boil (in mesh bag)
5 pounds medium shrimp, frozen or fresh, shelled, drained, and cleaned (save shells)
5 pounds frozen crab legs or 1 pound frozen crabmeat
48 oysters (save the liquid)
4 chicken breasts or 2 ½-pound whole chicken
2 pounds creole, kielbasa, or any smoked sausage cut into bite-size rounds
3 large onions, chopped
2 green peppers, chopped
6 scallions (green onions), chopped
6 cloves garlic, minced
2 32-ounce cans creole or stewed tomatoes
4 tablespoons butter
4 tablespoons flour
¼ cup chopped fresh parsley or 4 teaspoons dried parsley
2 bay leaves
1 teaspoon thyme
2 tablespoons Worcestershire sauce
½ teaspoon cayenne or chili peppers
1 teaspoon ground black pepper (optional)
3 pounds fresh or 4 10-ounce packages frozen okra
3 tablespoons hot pepper sauce
filé powder to taste
salt to taste
6 quarts or more stock (directions follow)

To make stock: boil chicken, ham, and shrimp-and-crab-boil bag in at least 12 cups water till cooked. Remove chicken and ham and set aside. Add shrimp shells to water and cook 30 minutes. Remove and discard shells.

Remove skin and bones from chicken and discard. Dice chicken. Add onion, pepper, scallions (green onions), garlic, and tomatoes to stock. Cook until onion is wilted and transparent, about 5 minutes. Add diced chicken and ham to stockpot.

Prepare roux: melt 4 tablespoons butter in a heavy pan or skillet over medium heat. When butter is hot, add 4 tablespoons flour all at once; stir or whisk quickly to combine butter and flour. Use back of spoon to smooth out any lumps. Reduce heat to low. Cook, stirring or whisking constantly till roux is dark brown.

Remove some broth from stockpot and add to roux. Continue cooking, stirring till broth is thickened to consistency of gravy. Return thickened broth to pot. Add parsley, bay leaves, thyme, Worcestershire sauce, cayenne, black pepper, and sausage. Simmer 10 minutes. Add oysters and their liquid, shrimp, and crabmeat or crab legs. Cook on medium heat 10 minutes. Add okra, hot sauce, filé powder, and salt. Continue cooking until seafood is thoroughly cooked.

Serve over steamed rice. The gumbo freezes well. It must be thoroughly cooled before freezing, however.

Jerrett Irons—All-American linebacker in 1996, he finished his career second on Michigan's all-time tackles list. Irons, one of only 11 Wolverines to start 40 or more games in his career, was an all-Big Ten pick in both 1995 and 1996.

Turkey Loaf

Desmond Howard

2 pounds ground turkey
1 cup bread crumbs
½ cup uncooked oatmeal
1 minced onion (fresh)
1 egg
¼ quart ketchup
1 small can tomato sauce

Mix everything in a large bowl and then place in a meat loaf container. Preheat oven to 350°. Place in the oven for about 1½ hours. Remove and let cool.

Desmond Howard—Michigan's second-ever Heisman Trophy winner, in 1991. All three Wolverine teams Howard played on won the Big Ten title. A receiver, Howard also made his mark on Michigan history with dazzling punt and kick returns. In 1997 Howard became the fourth man in history to win both the Heisman Trophy and the Super Bowl MVP Award.

Keftedes (Greek Meatballs)

Arthur Balourdos

2 pounds hamburger
2 teaspoons garlic powder
salt and pepper to taste
3 tablespoons vinegar
3 tablespoons water
5 tablespoons olive oil
2 tablespoons finely chopped dried mint
1 onion, finely chopped
2 tablespoons Parmesan cheese
2 eggs
¾ cup bread crumbs

Mix thoroughly, form into small hamburger-shaped patties, coat with flour. In a large pan, fry in very hot oil until cooked and browned on both sides.

Arthur Balourdos—The Chicago native started all 12 games at center during Michigan's 1984 season. A four-time letter winner, Baldouros was a Big Ten honorable mention selection in 1984.

Turkey Lasagna Rolls

David Hall

8 ounces ground turkey
1 medium onion chopped (½ cup)
2 cloves garlic, minced
1 cup water
1 7½-ounce can (⅔cup) tomatoes, cut up
1 6-ounce can tomato paste
1½ teaspoons dried oregano, crushed
1 teaspoon dried basil, crushed
8 packaged, dried lasagna noodles
1 beaten egg
1 15-ounce carton ricotta cheese
1 10-ounce package frozen chopped spinach, thawed and drained
1½ cups shredded mozzarella cheese
1 cup grated Parmesan cheese
fresh parsley sprigs (optional)

For sauce, in a large skillet cook turkey, onion, and garlic till turkey is no longer pink; drain fat. Stir in mushrooms, water, undrained tomatoes, tomato paste, oregano, and basil. Bring to boil; reduce heat. Cover and simmer for 25 minutes. Meanwhile, cook lasagna noodles according to package directions. Drain noodles twice; rinse with cold water.

For filling, in a mixing bowl stir together egg, ricotta cheese, spinach, 1 cup of the mozzarella cheese, and ¾ cup of the Parmesan cheese. Spread about ½ cup of the filling on each lasagna noodle. Starting from a narrow end, roll up each lasagna noodle. Place lasagna rolls in 2 quart rectangular baking dish. Pour sauce over lasagna rolls. Cover dish with foil.

Bake at 375° for 25 minutes. Remove foil. Sprinkle with remaining mozzarella cheese. Bake for 5-10 minutes more or till heated through. Let stand 5 minutes before serving. Sprinkle with remaining Parmesan cheese and, if desired, garnish with parsley sprigs. Makes 8 main dish servings or 16 appetizer servings.

Note: this recipe is great with or without turkey.

Poppy Seed Chicken

Rick Leach

- 4 *chicken breasts*
- 1 *can cream of chicken soup*
- 8 *ounces sour cream*
- 1 *can mushrooms*
- 1 *sleeve package Ritz crackers, crushed*
- 1 *tablespoon poppy seeds*
- ½ *stick butter, melted*

Boil chicken 40 minutes; drain. Cut chicken into bite-size pieces; line bottom of a 9″ x 9″ pan. Combine next 3 items together; pour over chicken. Combine crushed crackers with poppy seeds and melted butter; spoon over top of soup layer. Bake at 350° for 30 minutes or until bubbles.

Rick Leach—A four-year starter at quarterback, Leach played every game in which he was eligible. He led Michigan to three straight Big Ten titles from 1976 to 1978 and was named an all-American his senior season. A three-time all-Big Ten pick, Leach finished in the top 10 in the Heisman voting twice in his career.

Delmarva "Go Blue" (Crabs)

Bruce Getzan

- 1 *dozen (live!) Delaware, Maryland, New Jersey, or Virginia Go Blue crabs (in season usually May-October; Louisiana crabs may be substituted in the off-season)*
- 1 *can or bottle Labatt's Blue Beer*
- ½ *cup of vinegar*
- 1-2 *cups water (depending on size of the pot)*
- *generous amount Old Bay seasoning*

Pour water, vinegar, and Labatt's into a large pot. Place inverted steamer grate at the bottom of the pot. Top of liquid should be just under the inverted steamer grate. Bring to a boil. Add live crabs one at a time. Be sure to use glove or tongs (just as if you were shaking hands with Buckeyes, Gophers, Badgers, Nitnay Lions, etc.). Cover and steam until ripe for pickin'. The crabs will turn an orange-rose (bowl) color usually in 15-20 minutes, depending on their size. Place on a blue tray and resprinkle with Old Bay seasoning. Add steamed or boiled maize (corn on the cob) around the crabs for a true Maize and Go Blue! event. Repeat as necessary to feed the growing throng of Go Blue fans!

Baked Ham Sandwiches

Jason Bossard

1 pound sliced honey-cured ham
¼ pound butter
¼ cup chopped onion
¼ teaspoon horseradish mustard
1 teaspoon poppy seeds
1 dozen hamburger buns or rolls (onion rolls taste best)

Mix ingredients and spread on both halves of hamburger buns. Place one slice of Swiss cheese and sliced ham between bun halves. Wrap in foil. Bake at 350° for 20 minutes.

Jason Bossard—A letter winner on Michigan's basketball teams in 1991 through 1993, this outstanding guard guided the team to two NCAA championship games.

Mishmash

Mike Griffin

½ pound fresh spinach (or 10-ounce package frozen)
1 onion, chopped
1 clove garlic, minced
1 tablespoon oil
1 tablespoon butter
1 pound ground beef
½ teaspoon basil
1 teaspoon salt
¼ teaspoon freshly ground pepper
2 egg whites
1 can pitted black olives, chopped with liquid

If using fresh spinach, cook until just tender. Squeeze cooked or thawed spinach until rid of excess moisture. Chop. Heat oil and butter in a large heavy skillet. Sauté onion and garlic until soft. Add beef and brown. Sprinkle with basil, salt, and pepper. Stir in spinach. Keeping heat high, add egg whites to skillet, constantly stirring and lifting until egg whites are cooked. Add chopped olives plus juice, stir occasionally for 5 minutes. Serve immediately.

Pita breads that have been split, buttered, and sprinkled with Parmesan cheese, then broiled, are perfect with this.

Mike Griffin—The starting guard on Michigan's 1988–90 NCAA Champion basketball team, Griffin played four years for the Wolverines. A two-time academic all-American selection, he still ranks in Michigan's top 10, with 291 career assists.

Salmon Burgers

Chris Webber

1 15½- ounce can salmon
1 egg, beaten
¾ cup quick-cooking rolled oats
½ cup chopped onion
1 tablespoon chopped parsley
1 teaspoon prepared mustard
⅓ teaspoon salt
1 tablespoon lemon juice
dash pepper
cooking oil (if preparing on stove)

Drain the salmon. Combine with egg, oats, onion, parsley, lemon juice, mustard, salt, and pepper. Form into four patties, the size to fit on a hamburger bun. If grilling on an outdoor barbecue, it is a good idea to place a piece of foil under the burgers. If sautéing in a frying pan, use a small amount of cooking oil.

Matchless Meat Loaf

Chris Webber

- *1 ½ pounds ground beef*
- *1 ½ cups fresh bread crumbs*
- *¼ cup minced onion*
- *2 tablespoons finely cut parsley*
- *1 egg*
- *½ cup Coca-Cola (room temperature and stirred for accurate measurement)*
- *2 tablespoons catsup*
- *1 ½ tablespoons prepared salad mustard*
- *1 teaspoon salt*
- *½ teaspoon basil leaves*
- *⅛ teaspoon pepper*

In a bowl, break up meat with a fork; add crumbs, onion, and parsley, mixing well. Beat egg, mix with remaining ingredients. Pour over meat. With fork, toss lightly to blend thoroughly. Mixture will be soft. Turn into a 9″ x 5″ x 3″ loaf pan. Bake in a moderate oven, 350°, 1 hour. Let set about 10 minutes before slicing. Makes 6 to 8 servings.

Chris Webber—A member of Michigan's Fab Five recruiting class in 1991, Webber advanced to the NCAA championship game in both of his years at Michigan. Second on Michigan's all-time list in blocked shots. Currently an NBA all-star for the Washington Bullets.

Reuben Casserole

Neal Morton

- 2 *cups sauerkraut, rinsed and drained*
- ½ *teaspoon caraway seed*
- ½ *pound corned beef, sliced thin and broken into bite-size pieces*
- ¾ *cup mayonnaise*
- ¼ *cup Thousand Island dressing*
- 2 *large tomatoes, sliced thin*
- 2 *cups Swiss cheese, shredded*
- 6 *slices dark rye bread, crumbled*
- 2 *tablespoons butter or margarine, melted*

Spread sauerkraut in bottom of buttered casserole. Sprinkle half of caraway seed over sauerkraut. Layer corned beef over sauerkraut and drizzle dressing over all. Layer tomato slices and cheese over dressing. Toss bread crumbs and remaining caraway seeds with butter and spread over cheese layer. Bake at 400° for 25 minutes.

Amyre's Best Meatballs in the World

Amyre Makupson

1 pound ground beef
1 pound ground veal
1 pound ground pork
salt and pepper
¾ cup ketchup
¾ cup grape jelly

Thoroughly mix the 3 meats together. Hand form into bite-size balls. Put equal amounts of jelly and ketchup in a pot. (You can use as much jelly and ketchup as you would like, as long as they are in equal proportions.) Bring to a boil. Put in meatballs. Simmer and let cook about an hour. Let cool. Refrigerate overnight. Skim fat from the top. Reheat and enjoy!

Amyre Makupson—Amyre is known as one of television's most active news anchors. Along with her duties as coanchor of WKBD's "Ten O'Clock News," she is executive producer and host of "Straight Talk," a weekly issue-oriented talk show. Amyre is also public affairs manager at the station. She is responsible for all editorials, public service announcements, and license-renewal procedures for WKBD.

Fourth Down Fajitas

David Scott

1 pound skirt steak (for two to four servings)
1 small bottle of Lea & Perrins Worcestershire sauce
⅛ cup ground cumin (to make it smoky)
1 tablespoon garlic powder
1 tablespoon ground pepper
2 yellow onions in thinly sliced rings
juice of 2 limes

Combine all ingredients and marinate overnight. Separate onions into foil on the grill. Cook meat on the grill to your taste. Load up flour tortilla with meat and onions, along with sour cream, Colby and Monterey cheeses, guacamole (all optional).

David Scott—This Emmy Award winning news anchor is a true blue fan. He and his wife are permanent fixtures at all of the UM home games. Not only does David enjoy the Wolverines on the field, but he also reports about them during the UPN-50 "Ten O'Clock News".

Salmon with creamy Horseradish Sauce

Laura Teicher

- ¼ *cup dry white table wine*
- 2 *tablespoons chopped onion*
- 1 *tablespoon lemon juice*
- 1 *teaspoon peppercorns*
- 2 *salmon steaks (whatever size you prefer)*
- 2 *tablespoons sour cream*
- 2 *tablespoons prepared horseradish*
- 1 *teaspoon all-purpose flour and chopped fresh mint*
- ¼ *teaspoon pepper*

Combine ½ cup water and wine with onion, lemon juice, and peppercorns. Cover it and cook until the mixture comes to a boil . Add the salmon (medium-low heat) and cover. Simmer until the salmon flakes easily when gently dragging a fork over it . How long it takes to cook will depend on the size of salmon you pick. While the salmon is cooking, prepare the horseradish mixture. In a small mixing bowl combine the sour cream, horseradish, flour, mint, and pepper. Stir and wait. Put your salmon on a serving platter and keep it warm. Drain the liquid it was cooking in through a sieve into a bowl. Throw away the solids. Return to the skillet and cook the liquid until it boils, then add the horseradish mixture. Reduce the heat to low and cook until the mixture thickens (about 2-3 minutes). Then pour it over the salmon. It's delicious.

Laura Teicher—Laura can be heard on WWJ-AM radio 950. Laura has been a radio reporter for 5 years.

Bourbon-Basted Turkey

Barry Alvarenz

- 4-8 *pounds turkey breast*
- ¾ *cup bourbon*
- ¾ *cup brown sugar*
- ¾ *cup soy sauce*
- 1 *pinch fresh ginger, chopped fine*
- 1-3 *cloves garlic, chopped fine*

Mix together bourbon, sugar, soy sauce, ginger, and garlic. Pour over turkey and marinate in Ziploc bag overnight. Put turkey and marinade in roasting pan and roast according to turkey-weight instructions, spooning marinade over turkey occasionally. Discard marinade before serving. Serve hot or cold.

Pizza Casserole

Don Nehlen

- 24 *ounces noodles*
- 2 *pounds ground chuck*
- 2 *large cans pizza sauce*
- 1½ *cans cheddar cheese soup*
- 1 *can mushrooms*
- *shredded mozzarella cheese*

Cook and drain noodles. Brown the ground chuck. Add pizza sauce and cheddar cheese soup. Mix. Add mushrooms and the drained noodles. Mix. Pour into a greased 9″ x 13″ pan. Cover with foil and bake at 350° for 45 minutes to 1 hour. Remove from oven and sprinkle shredded mozzarella cheese on top. Return to oven, uncovered, until cheese melts.

Chili

Lou Holtz

1½ pounds ground sirloin
2 cloves garlic
olive oil
3 tablespoons chili powder
1 15½-ounce can dark red kidney beans
1 46-ounce can V-8 juice
1 pound can whole tomatoes
15 ounces tomato sauce
15 ounces water

Brown garlic lightly in olive oil. Remove the garlic and set aside. Brown the sirloin in the garlic-flavored oil. Once the meat is browned, return garlic to mixture. Add all remaining ingredients except kidney beans. Simmer to desired thickness (about 1½ hours). Add kidney beans during the last half hour of cooking. If desired, sprinkle with shredded cheddar cheese or chopped onion.

Lou Holtz—There's not a Michigan player out there who hasn't worried about either a trip to South Bend or the Fighting Irish invading Michigan stadium. The Wolverines will be the first to tell you, either Holtz is just a very lucky coach or he is just one of the best to ever hit college football.

Sweet and Sour Meatballs

Lloyd Carr

1 pound ground beef
½ cup bread crumbs
¼ cup milk
1 teaspoon salt
⅛ teaspoon pepper
½ teaspoon Worcestershire sauce
12 ounces chili sauce
10 ounces grape jelly

Mix together and form into meatballs. Brown in saucepan, then add chili sauce and grape jelly.

Veggie Chicken Chili

Bill McCartney

¾ cup margarine
½ cup carrots
2 stalks celery, diced
¼ pound zucchini
¼ cup yellow onions
¼ cup diced green peppers
1 cup fresh mushrooms, sliced
8 cups chicken, diced
5 cups diced tomatoes in puree
4 15-ounce cans great northern beans
2 15-ounce cans black beans
½ cup diced green chilies
1 tablespoon chili powder
¼ teaspoon white pepper
1 teaspoon black pepper
1 teaspoon celery salt
½ teaspoon salt
1½ teaspoons garlic, minced
1 tablespoon basil
1 tablespoon ground cumin
4 15-ounce cans Mexican or southwest chili tomatoes
½ cup whole black olives, pitted
½ cup shredded Monterey Jack cheese
½ cup grated Parmesan cheese

Sauté carrots, celery, zucchini, diced green onions, yellow onions, diced green peppers, mushrooms, and chicken until soft and chicken is no longer pink. Add remaining ingredients except cheeses. Bring to boil; reduce heat and simmer 40 minutes. Add cheeses and simmer 5 minutes more. Makes 1 gallon.

Flame's Hot 'n Spicy Chicken Barbecue

John Arbeznik

- ½ *cup A•1 steak sauce*
- ½ *cup tomato sauce*
- ¼ *cup finely chopped onion*
- 2 *teaspoons cider vinegar*
- 2 *teaspoons maple syrup*
- 1 *teaspoon vegetable oil*
- 3 *teaspoons chili powder*
- ½ *teaspoon crushed red pepper flakes*
- 1 *3-pound chicken, cut up*

In a medium saucepan, combine steak sauce, tomato sauce, onion, vinegar, maple syrup, oil, chili powder, and red pepper flakes. Over medium heat, heat to a boil; reduce heat. Simmer 5 to 7 minutes or until thickened. Cool.

Grill chicken over medium heat 30 to 40 minutes or until done, turning and basting frequently with prepared sauce. Serve hot.

John Arbeznik—An offensive guard on Michigan's Big Ten Championship teams of 1977 and 1978, Arbeznik was an all-Big Ten pick in 1978–79. The University Heights, Ohio, native started 22 games in his three-year Michigan career.

Tzimmes

Alex Agase

- 2 *pounds short ribs or stew meat*
- 1½ *pounds carrots, peeled and sliced*
- 5 *sweet potatoes, cut into quarters*
- 4 *small white or red potatoes, peeled and sliced*
- 12 *prunes, pitted*
- 1 *onion, sliced*
- ½ *cup brown sugar*
- *salt to taste*

Preheat oven to 300°. Put meat in pot of water to cover. Bring to boil, uncovered. Remove foam. Add salt; add onions. Simmer 10 minutes. Add carrots (make sure water covers). Cook 10 minutes on medium heat. Add potatoes and sugar; cook 20 minutes longer. Put into a 4-quart casserole; cover. Add prunes. Bake in oven at 300° for 40 minutes. Serves 8-10.

Alex Agase—Alex was a three time all-American football player at Purdue and Illinois. He played six seasons in the NFL and was inducted into the College Football Hall of Fame. He has served as the head coach at Northwestern and Purdue, athletic director at Eastern Michigan University and volunteer coach at UM.

Slightly Spicy! Original Spaghetti Sauce

Dan Heikkinen

- 1 *large can Hunt's tomato sauce*
- 1 *teaspoon parsley flakes*
- 2 *dashes garlic salt*
- 2 *dashes black pepper*
- 1 *teaspoon oregano*
- 1 *teaspoon basil*
- 1 *tablespoon Original Open Pit barbecue sauce*
- *up to a pound of browned ground chuck (optional)*

Mix all the ingredients into a bowl. Let sit overnight, if possible, to allow the tomato and barbecue sauces to get a good flavor. Heat on a low temperature for 1 hour. Stir frequently.

Dan Heikkinen—All-American letter winner in track and cross-country, he was 1989 10,000-meter outdoor Big Ten Champion and 1981 indoor 20-mile Big Ten Champion.

Polynesian Chicken

Dan Dierdorf

1 cut-up chicken
1 8-ounce bottle Russian or mild French dressing
1 jar (8–12 ounces) apricot preserves
1 package dry onion soup mix

Line 9″ x 13″ pan with tinfoil. Place chicken in one layer in pan. Mix remaining ingredients and spoon over chicken. Bake, uncovered, at 300°-325° about 1½ hours, stirring and basting with sauce occasionally.

Fusillo Pizzaiolo

Elvis Grbac

8 ounces sliced mushrooms
1 large red pepper
1 large green pepper
10 green onions, chopped
1 large onion, diced
1 clove garlic, chopped
3 large shallots
½ cup fresh basil
2 tablespoons fresh oregano
dash ground red pepper
¼ cup olive oil
4 cups chopped canned tomatoes
salt and pepper to taste
16 ounces fusillo
2 tablespoons chopped parsley

Sauté first 10 ingredients in oil until lightly browned. Add tomatoes. Bring to boil. Simmer for 20 minutes. Season with salt and pepper. Serve over cooked pasta.

Chicken Enchiladas

Bill McCartney

Sauce

2 10-ounce cans cream of chicken soup
1 cup sour cream
¼ teaspoon garlic salt
2 4-ounce cans chopped green chilies

Combine and set aside.

Filling

3 cups grated cheddar or longhorn cheese
3 cups chopped cooked chicken
½ cup chopped green onions
12 flour tortillas

Combine cheese, chicken, onions, and about one third of sauce mixture; mix until moist. Place half cup of filling mixture in center of each tortilla. Spread mixture over tortilla and roll up. Place, seam side down, in baking dish. Pour remaining sauce over rolled enchiladas, covering well.

Bake 30 minutes at 350° until melted thoroughly. Serves 8.

Elegant Chicken

John Cooper

- *4-6 chicken breasts*
- *½ package Good Seasons Italian dressing*
- *1 can cream of mushroom soup*
- *1 container whipped cream cheese and chives*
- *⅓ cup white wine*
- *2 tablespoons butter*

Melt butter, add dressing. Brown chicken in this mixture and place in 9" x 13" Pyrex dish. Mix cream cheese, soup, and wine, pour over chicken. Bake uncovered at 350° for 45 minutes. Baste once.

John Cooper—Her has followed in the steps of some legendary coaches at Ohio State. One that comes to everyone's mind—Woody Hayes. Cooper has continued Hayes' fine tradition at the school, and has also continued the fierce competition in the Big Ten against their top rival, the Wolverines.

Chicken Parmesan

Paul Heuerman

2 cups bread crumbs
1 cup Parmesan cheese
1 tablespoon salt
⅓ cup fresh parsley
1 clove garlic, crushed
1 tablespoon Dijon mustard
1½ teaspoons Worcestershire sauce
½ pound butter or margarine, melted
6 chicken breasts, halved and boned

Mix crumbs, cheese, salt, and parsley. Add garlic, mustard, and Worcestershire sauce to the melted butter. Dip chicken in the butter mixture, then in crumbs. Place in a large shallow pan and drizzle with remaining butter. Bake in a 300° oven for 1¼ hours.

Paul Heuerman—The starting center for the 1980–81 Wolverine basketball team, which advanced to the NIT. Heuerman was a four-year letter winner who earned second-team Academic all-American honors in 1981.

Fourth Quarter
Desserts and Beverages

My Mama's Apple Cake

Bo Schembechler (Millie's)

- 1 *cup cooking oil*
- 2 *cups sugar*
- 3 *eggs*
- 2¼ *cups flour, sifted*
- 1 *teaspoon soda*
- 1 *teaspoon vanilla*
- 3 *cups apple, sliced*
- 1 *cup pecans, chopped*

Cream oil, sugar, and eggs. Add flour and soda. Add vanilla, apples, and pecans. Bake in tube pan for 1 hour at 350°.

Chocolate Mound Cookies (Haystacks)

Bo Schembechler (Millie's)

12 ounces chocolate chips
12 ounces butterscotch chips
1 5½-ounce can chow mein noodles
1 large can cocktail peanuts

Melt chips, add noodles and peanuts. Stir till well covered. Drop by spoonful on cookie sheet. Cool short time in freezer or refrigerator.

Double Chocolate Chip Cookies

President Gerald Ford

1 *cup of butter*
1¾ *cups sugar*
2 *eggs*
2 *teaspoons brandy or vanilla extract*
1 *ounce unsweetened baking chocolate*
¼ *cup sour cream*
2 *cups unbleached all-purpose flour*
¾ *cup cocoa*
½ *teaspoon baking soda*
¼ *teaspoon baking powder*
½ *teaspoon salt*
12 *ounces white chocolate, chopped (2 cups)*
1 *cup chopped shelled Brazil nuts or almonds*

Beat the butter and sugar together until light and fluffy. Beat in the eggs, one at a time. Beat in the brandy. Melt the chocolate in a dish over hot water. Stir the melted chocolate and sour cream into the creamed mixture.

Sift together the flour, cocoa, baking soda, baking powder, and salt. Stir the dry ingredients gradually into the melted chocolate mixture to form a batter. Stir in the white chocolate chips and nuts. Drop the batter by tablespoons onto ungreased cookie sheet. Bake at 350° for 10 minutes. Makes about 5 dozen.

Pineapple Squares

John Wangler

Crust

3 cups flour
⅓ cup butter or margarine
1 cup sugar
⅓ cup milk
3 teaspoons baking powder
1 teaspoon vanilla
2 eggs
1 teaspoon salt

Cream shortening and sugar, set aside. Mix eggs, vanilla, and milk; add to sugar mixture. Combine flour, baking powder, and salt. Add flour, one cup at a time, to the sugar-egg mixture. Mix until crust can be formed into a ball. Form 2 balls and chill in the refrigerator for 1 hour.

Filling

1 can crushed pineapple (No. 2 size)
½ cup sugar
½ teaspoon salt
4 tablespoons cornstarch
¼ cup cold water

Mix together in a heavy saucepan, heat to a boil. Stir constantly (burns easily). Roll crust on a pastry cloth that has been well rubbed with flour and powdered sugar. Roll out two crusts (top and bottom crust) that will fit into a medium-sized cookie sheet.

Carefully spread filling onto the bottom crust.

Cover filling with top crust. Crimp edges to seal. Pierce top crust in a few places with a fork. Bake in a preheated 375° oven for 30 to 35 minutes. When cool, sprinkle with powdered sugar. Cut into diamond shapes.

Chocolate Chip Oatmeal Cookies

Leroy Hoard

1 cup butter
1 cup brown sugar
1 cup white sugar
2 eggs
2 teaspoons vanilla
½ teaspoon salt
1 teaspoon baking powder
1 teaspoon baking soda
2 cups flour
2½ cups oatmeal
½ Hershey bar (ground up, mix in oatmeal)
1 12-ounce bag chocolate chips

Mix butter, brown sugar, and white sugar. Add eggs and vanilla. Stir in salt, baking powder, baking soda, and flour. Stir in oatmeal, Hershey bar, and chocolate chips. Place golf ball size or smaller cookies 2" apart on ungreased cookie sheet. Bake at 325°-350° for 10-13 minutes.

Leroy Hoard—The tailback ran for over 1,500 yards from 1987 to 1989 as the Wolverines advanced to the Rose Bowl twice. He garnered honorable mention all-Big Ten honors in 1989, gaining 152 yards against Ohio State to give Michigan the Big Ten title.

Potato Chip Cookies

Andy Cannavino

- *1 pound butter*
- *1 cup sugar*
- *3 cups flour*
- *1 cup walnuts, chopped*
- *2 cups crushed potato chips*
- *2 teaspoons vanilla*

Cream butter and sugar together, add vanilla. Sift flour twice and then remeasure and then add flour and walnuts. Fold in crushed potato chips. Bake on ungreased cookie sheet, one teaspoon of dough makes one cookie (do not ball), 350° for about 12 minutes.

Andy Cannavino—A three-year letter winner for the Wolverines (1978–80). Cannavino was an all-Big Ten pick at linebacker in 1980. Captain of Michigan's 1980 squad, which won the Big Ten title and went to the Rose Bowl. Cannavino was selected to play in the 1981 Hula Bowl.

Aunt Rozella's Sour Cream Coffee Cake

Dick Kempthorn

¾ cup firmly packed brown sugar
¾ cup chopped walnuts or pecans
1 full teaspoon ground cinnamon
1½ cups all-purpose flour
1½ teaspoons baking powder
½ teaspoon baking soda
½ cup (1 stick) unsalted butter, room temperature
1½ cups sugar
3 eggs
1 cup sour cream
1½ teaspoons vanilla

Mix and set aside brown sugar, nuts, and cinnamon. Preheat oven to 350°. Grease tube pan (angel food cake pan). In a separate bowl, sift together flour, baking powder, and baking soda. In a separate bowl, using electric mixer beat butter and sugar until fluffy, then beat in eggs one at a time until just combined (do not overbeat). Mix in sour cream and vanilla. Add flour mixture and stir until blended. Spoon half of batter into prepared pan. Sprinkle half of brown sugar mixture over and swirl gently into batter, using a small knife. Spoon remaining brown sugar mixture over and blend slightly. Bake until tester comes out clean, about 1 hour. Cool in pan 10 minutes. Cut around pan to loosen cake, turn out onto rack, and cool completely.

Orange Slush Supreme

James Bolden

- 2 *6-ounce cans frozen lemonade*
- 1 *6-ounce can frozen orange juice.*
- 2 *cups sugar*
- 7 *cups water*
- 2 *cups strong tea (4 tea bags brewed in 2 cups water)*
- 1 *cup whiskey*

Mix ingredients and freeze.

James Bolden—Bolden started 23 games as a defensive back for Michigan from 1974 to 1976. The native of Akron, Ohio, was an honorable mention all-Big Ten selection during his senior year as the Wolverines advanced to the Rose Bowl.

Raspberry Pie

Jim Breaugh

Crust

1½ cups vanilla wafer crumbs
¼ cup butter, melted

Mix to make crust, save ¼ cup for topping.

First Layer

½ cup butter
1½ cups confectioners' sugar
2 eggs

Cream butter, gradually add sugar. Add eggs one at a time and beat mixture until light and fluffy. Spread over crust and chill.

Second Layer

½ cup sugar
2 tablespoons cornstarch
1 10-ounce package frozen raspberries, thawed

Combine sugar and cornstarch. Add raspberries and cook over medium heat stirring constantly until thick and clear. Cool, then pour over first layer.

Whipped Cream Topping
- *1 cup whipping cream*
- *¼ cup confectioners' sugar*
- *1 teaspoon vanilla*

Beat cream until stiff, fold in sugar and vanilla. Sprinkle with remaining crumbs. Chill several hours.

Jim Breaugh—A quarterback for Michigan in 1977, the West Bloomfield, Michigan, native was a football, basketball, and baseball player in high school.

Chocolate Puzzle Bars

Paul Heuerman

- 2 *cups flour*
- 1½ *cups brown sugar*
- 1 *large package instant chocolate pudding*
- ¾ *cup butter*
- 1 *large package chocolate chips*
- 1 *cup milk*
- ½ *cup chopped walnuts*

Crust

Crumble flour, brown sugar, and butter together. Put ½ of mixture into an 8″ x 12″ pan. Pat down. Bake 10 minutes.

Filling

Mix instant chocolate pudding, chocolate chips, and milk on slow burner. Cook and stir until thick. Add chopped walnuts. Pour over crust. Sprinkle remainder of crust on filling. Bake at 350° for 20 minutes.

Fourth Down and Bundt Cake

George Lilja

1 *box devil's food cake mix*
1½ *cups sour cream*
¾ *cup vegetable oil*
½ *cup Kahlúa*
2 *eggs (beat with fork)*
1 *3.4-ounce package instant vanilla pudding*

Mix all together with a big spoon and leave lumpy. Bake at 350° in a greased and floured bundt cake pan for 45 minutes. Cool. Dust top with powdered sugar. A very rich, moist cake. Isn't messy, so no forks or plates needed. Easy!

Banana Oatmeal Cookies

Lou Tepper

1½ cups flour
1 teaspoon salt
½ teaspoon baking soda
½ teaspoon nutmeg
¾ teaspoon cinnamon
¾ cup butter
1 cup sugar
1 egg
2 cups ripe banana
1 teaspoon vanilla
1½ cups raw oats
1 cup raisins

Mix dry ingredients and set aside. Beat sugar, egg, and butter. Add bananas and vanilla, then mix in dry ingredients.

Drop by tablespoon on an ungreased cookie sheet. Bake at 400° for 12 minutes. Makes about 3 dozen.

Lou Tepper—Tepper started coaching for the Fighting Illini in 1988. His main job there was defensive coordinator. Tepper then moved into the assistant coaching job and in 1994 accepted the head coaching job at the University of Illinois. Tepper had directed Illinois to victories over every Big Ten school except Penn State, beating Michigan in Ann Arbor in 1993, Ohio State in Columbus in 1992 and 1994, and Wisconsin in Madison in 1992.

Robbie's Coffee Cake

Robbie Timmons

1 stick butter
1½ cups sugar
2 eggs
1 cup sour cream
1 teaspoon vanilla
2 cups flour
1½ teaspoons baking powder
1 teaspoon baking soda
1 cup nuts
1 teaspoon cinnamon

Melt butter; cool. Mix with 1 cup sugar (save ½ cup for later), eggs, sour cream, and vanilla until well blended. Mix in flour combined with baking powder and soda. Pour into an 8″ or 9″ pan. Mix nuts with remaining sugar and cinnamon; swirl into batter. Bake 1 hour at 350°. Makes 9 servings or more.

Robbie Timmons—Even though this WXYZ-TV newsanchor is a Buckeye, she soon turned into a maize and blue fan when she married former UM football player Jim Brandstatter. You can catch Robbie during home games in Ann Arbor—her husband Jim has a new career off the field as the voice of Wolverine sports.

Orange Cake

Joe Paterno

1 large Florida orange
1 cup raisins
⅓ cup walnuts
½ cup vegetable shortening
1 cup sugar
2 large eggs
2 cups flour
1 teaspoon baking soda
1 teaspoon salt
1 cup milk

Squeeze ⅓ cup juice from orange; reserve for orange-nut topping. Remove any seeds from orange. Place unpeeled orange, raisins, and nuts in blender or food processo; process until finely ground. Set aside. In a large mixer bowl, cream shortening and sugar. Beat in eggs. Combine flour, baking soda, and salt. Add to creamed mixture alternately with milk. Fold orange-raisin mixture into batter. Spread batter into a greased and floured 13″ x 9″ x 2″ baking disk. Bake in a preheated 350° oven 40 to 50 minutes. Cool 10 minutes.

Topping

- *⅓ cup sugar*
- *¼ cup chopped walnuts*
- *1 teaspoon ground cinnamon*

Drizzle reserved ⅓cup orange juice over warm cake. Combine sugar, walnuts, and cinnamon, sprinkle over cake. Garnish with whole walnuts and orange slices, if desired. Yield: 20 servings.

Joe Paterno—Paterno has been head coach at Penn State University for 31 years, compiling a record of 288-74-3 in that span. His teams have been to 27 bowl games. He is a graduate of Brown University.

Rhubarb Custard Pie

Kimberly Voet

1 11-ounce package pie crust mix
2½ cups unpared rhubarb, cut into 1″ lengths
1½ cups sugar
¼ cup flour
2 eggs, slightly beaten
2 teaspoons lemon juice
dash salt
2 tablespoons butter
1 tablespoon sugar

Make pastry as package directs. Handling gently, shape into ball. Divide in half; form each into a round, then flatten with palm of hand. On lightly floured pastry cloth, roll half of pastry into 12″ circle. Roll with light strokes from center to edge, lifting rolling pin as you reach edge.

Place a 9″ pie plate on pastry circle (pastry should be 1″ wider all around). Fold pastry in half and carefully transfer to pie plate, making sure fold is in center of pie plate. Unfold pastry and fit it carefully into pie plate, pressing gently with fingers so pastry fits snugly all around (do not stretch). Refrigerate. Preheat oven to 450°.

In a large bowl, combine rhubarb, sugar, flour, eggs, lemon juice, salt. Turn into lined pie plate. Dot with butter.

Roll out remaining pastry into 12″ circle. Fold over in quarters; cut slits for steam vents. Using scissors, trim overhanging pastry to measure ½″ from rim of pie plate. Carefully place folding pastry so that point is at the center of filling, and unfold. Using scissors, trim overhanging pastry of top crust to measure 1″ from edge all around. Moisten edge of bottom pastry with a little water. Fold top pastry under edge of bottom pastry. With fingers, press edges together to seal, so juices cannot run out. Press upright to form a standing rim. Crimp edge decoratively.

Sprinkle with 1 tablespoon sugar. Bake at 450° for 10 minutes. Reduce heat to 350° and bake 30 minutes. Serves 6.

Kim Voet—This producer for WDIV-TV's Nightbeat can be found at every Wolverine home game. A well-known fanatic, Kim has spent her broadcast career following her favorite Meeechigan *team while she spent time producing the news in various markets around the country. Now that she's back in her favorite state—look out Wolverines, your #1 fan is on the sidelines.*

Lemon Bars (aka Maize Bars)

Beth Nissen

2 cups sifted all-purpose flour
½ cup confectioners' sugar
1 cup margarine
4 beaten eggs
2 cups granulated sugar
⅓ cup lemon juice
¼ cup all-purpose flour
½ teaspoon baking powder

Sift together 2 cups flour and confectioners' sugar. Cut in margarine till mixture clings together. Press into a 13" x 9" x 2" baking pan. Bake at 350° for 20-25 minutes or until lightly browned. Beat together eggs, granulated sugar, and lemon juice. Sift together the flour and the baking powder. Stir in egg mixture. Pour over baked crust. Bake in preheated oven at 350° for 25 minutes longer. Dust warm with confectioners' sugar.

Beth Nissen—We see her reports from around the globe on ABC news every night. But how many of you know that Beth is not only a UM alum, but actually grew up watching the Wolverines play in her hometown of Ann Arbor? Beth has worked at televisions stations all across the U.S., but professes that she is glued to the set whenever her favorite team hits the airwaves.

Caramel Layer Choc-Square

Harlan Huckelby

1 12-ounce can evaporated milk
1 package Kraft caramels
1 package German or Swiss chocolate cake mix
1 cup nuts, chopped
1 6-ounce bag chocolate chips
¾ cup margarine, melted

Mix together 4 ounces evaporated milk and caramels. Cook in a double boiler, stirring often, until mixture is smooth. Set aside. Stir together cake mix, margarine, remaining evaporated milk, and nuts.

Press half of the dough into the bottom of a greased 13" x 9" x 2" baking pan. Bake at 350° for 6 to 8 minutes. Sprinkle chocolate chips on baked dough and top with melted caramel mixture. Crumble remaining dough on top and return to oven. Continue baking 15 to 18 minutes. Cool and cut into bars.

Harlan Huckelby—Harlan began his successful Wolverine career in 1975. Huck, the nickname his teamates gave him, was a world-class sprinter at Detroit's Cass Tech High School. The speedster set numerous records in his athletic career. He was drafted in 1979 by the New Orleans Saints.

Chocolate Delight

Rich Hewlett

1 package Jiffy brownie mix
⅓ cup Kahlúa
8 ounces Cool Whip
1 package Jell-O instant chocolate pudding
4 Heath bars

Bake brownies according to directions on the box; cool. Pierce holes into brownies with a fork and pour Kahlúa over top. Set aside. Prepare pudding according to directions. Break Heath bars into small pieces using food processor. Break up the brownies and layer with pudding, Cool Whip and Heath bar.

Rich Hewlett—Rich began his maize and blue career in 1979. He started the Ohio State game as a freshman quarterback. Rich was known as one of Michigan's best holders and option quaterbacks in the history of UM football. Rich continues his succcess off the field as a prominent business attorney. We'll probably see him in the spotlight as a future supreme court justice.

Harvey Wallbanger Cake

Jim Brandstatter

- 1 *box orange supreme or yellow cake mix*
- 1 *box (4-serving size) instant vanilla pudding*
- ½ *cup oil*
- ¾ *cup orange juice*
- 4 *eggs*
- ¼ *cup Galliano*
- ¼ *cup vodka*

Combine all ingredients well and pour into a bundt pan sprayed with cooking spray. Bake 45-55 minutes at 350°.

Jim Brandstatter—Even though Jim came from East Lansing, it didn't take long for his maize and blue colors to show through. He started his football career at Michigan as offensive tackle on Michigan's 1969-71 teams. He started ten games at right tackle in 1971, when Michigan went to the Rose Bowl. Currently the television host of both UM basketball and football coaches shows.

Chocolate Peanut Butter Cookie Bars

Bernie Smilovitz

1 package Pillsbury yellow cake mix
1 cup peanut butter
½ cup butter or margarine, melted
2 eggs

Filling
1 cup semisweet chocolate pieces
1⅓ cup (14-ounce can) sweetened condensed milk
2 tablespoons butter or margarine
1 package Pillsbury coconut pecan or coconut almond frosting mix

In a large bowl, combine cake mix, peanut butter, margarine, and eggs. Mix by hand, stir until dough holds together. Press two-thirds of dough into bottom of an ungreased 13" x 9" baking pan. Reserve remaining dough for topping. Set aside. In a saucepan, combine chocolate pieces, milk, butter. Melt over low heat, stirring until smooth. Remove from heat; stir in frosting mix.

Spoon filling over the dough in baking pan. Crumble reserved dough over filling. Bake at 350° for 20-25 minutes. Cool and cut into bars. Makes 36 bars.

Bernie Smilovitz—Bernie's back from his stint at WCBS sports in New York to cover the games for WDIV. The nationally and locally award-winning sports journalist has covered many games at UM, everything from their run to the roses to coverage of Heisman winner Desmond Howard.

Cannoli Cake

Andy Cannavino

1 19-ounce package lemon cake mix
½ cup oil
4 eggs
1 cup milk
2 cups ricotta cheese
¾ cup sugar
½ teaspoon cinnamon
1 teaspoon vanilla
maraschino cherries

Preheat oven to 375°. Combine cake mix, oil, eggs, and milk and blend thoroughly; pour into a greased pan (either two 9″ round layer pans or one 11″ x 14″ pan). Bake layer 25-30 minutes, rectangle 30-35 minutes. Cake is done when it pops back after being lightly pressed with a finger. Cool.

Blend ricotta, sugar, cinnamon, and vanilla; mix well. Spread over cooled cake. Dot with maraschino cherries for color.

Homemade Kahlúa

Paul Seymour

3	*cups water*
3 ½	*cups sugar*
	instant coffee
1	*vanilla bean*
1	*pint water*
1	*pint grain alcohol*

Mix water and sugar and boil 10-20 minutes. Add 4 rounded tablespoons of instant coffee and vanilla bean (split lengthwise). Cool; add 1 pint water and 1 pint grain alcohol. Let sit 2 weeks with vanilla bean. Then remove bean.

Cheese Cookies

Jon Falk

- 2 *sticks margarine*
- 1 *8-ounce package cream cheese*
- 2¼ *cups flour, do not sift*

Mix margarine and cream cheese together until creamy. Then add flour. Mix all together; refrigerate overnight.

Separate dough into tiny balls. Roll balls in sugar, then flatten up and fill them with your favorite filling; fold them in half, and crease to make a seal.

You can add apricot, pineapple, date and nut fillings. All are good.

Bake at 350° for 20 minutes.

Jon Falk—A legend at the University of Michigan, he is approaching the silver anniversary mark as head equipment manager. Falk is known as one of the most respected equipment managers in the country, and has served as the executive director of the athletic equipment managers association for the past ten years.

Brownies

Red Berenson

1 cup water
½ cup buttermilk
2 sticks margarine or butter
4 tablespoons cocoa
1 teaspoon baking soda
2 cups unsifted flour
2 cups sugar
dash of salt
2 eggs
1 teaspoon vanilla

Mix together water, buttermilk, margarine, and cocoa on stove till boiling, then remove. Mix baking soda, flour, sugar, and salt, then combine with first mixture. Stir in eggs and vanilla. Pour into a greased and floured jelly roll pan or lasagna pan or 13″ x 9″ cake pan. Bake at 350° for 15-20 minutes.

Icing (start 10 minutes before cake is done)
4 tablespoons cocoa
1 stick margarine
6 tablespoons buttermilk
1 teaspoon vanilla
1 cup chopped pecans
1 pound box powdered sugar

Bring to boil cocoa, margarine, and buttermilk. Add vanilla, pecans, and powdered sugar. Cool cake 10 minutes on rack and pour icing over.

Pretzel Salad

Joe Roberson

First Layer

- *2 cups small curly pretzels, crushed*
- *¾ cup butter, melted*
- *2½ tablespoons sugar*

Mix together and spread in bottom of a 9″ x 13″ pan. Bake at 400° for 8 minutes.

Second Layer

- *8 ounces cream cheese, softened*
- *½ cup sugar*
- *1 medium-size carton of Cool Whip*

Mix together and spread on cooled pretzel crust.

Third Layer

- *6 ounces strawberry Jell-O*
- *2 cups boiling water*
- *2 10-ounce packages frozen strawberries*

Let Jell-O mixture partially set, then pour over cream cheese layer. Refrigerate till set.

Sour Cream Pound Cake

Jim Colletto

3 cups flour
3 cups sugar
6 eggs, separated
1 cup butter (2 sticks)
1 cup sour cream (half pint carton)
¼ teaspoon soda
2 teaspoons vanilla

Sift flour, then measure and sift again with soda. Beat egg whites and set aside. Cream butter and sugar well, then add egg yolks one at a time. Add vanilla. Beat. Add flour alternately with sour cream one-third at a time and beat each time. Fold in beaten egg whites last. Grease and flour a 10" tube pan. Pour mixture into tube pan and bake at 300° for 1½ hours until top is rather crispy.

Jim Coletto—Well known throughout the Big Ten for staging a big comeback for the Boilermakers, Coletto was a semifinalist for the 1994 Football News *National Coach of the Year. Under Coletto, the Boilermakers finished first in the Big Ten in rushing (233.4) offense in 1995, eighth nationally.*

Caramel Cookies

Butch Wolfolk

2 ½ cups flour
½ teaspoon baking powder
1 cup butter
¾ cup brown sugar, firmly packed
1 teaspoon vanilla
⅓ cup pecans, chopped fine
½ pound caramels (about 24)
¼ cup water

Sift together flour and baking powder; set aside. Melt butter in a 2-quart saucepan over low heat. Stir in brown sugar, vanilla, and pecans. Add the flour and baking powder. Shape dough into balls using a teaspoon; flatten and pinch tops to form an acorn. Bake at 350° for 15-18 minutes.

Melt caramels and water in top of a double boiler. Dip flat ends of cookies into caramel sauce and then into chopped pecans.

Cheese Strudel

Rob Lytle

2 packages Pillsbury crescent rolls
2 8-ounce packages cream cheese
1 egg
1 cup sugar
1 teaspoon vanilla
¼ cup margarine
½ cup flour

Beat cream cheese, egg, ¾ cup sugar, and vanilla until smooth. Set aside. Spread one package of the crescent rolls across the bottom of a 9″ x 13″ Pyrex baking dish. Spread cream cheese mixture evenly over the crescent-roll dough. Unroll the second package of crescent rolls over the layer of cheese. Mix remaining ¼ cup of sugar, margarine, and flour with a fork until doughy. Then crumble over top of crescent dough. Bake at 400° for 10 minutes, then reduce heat to 350° for 20 minutes. Don't let it get brown.

Mocha Cheesecake

Don Shane

Crust

1½ cups chocolate wafers, finely crushed
⅓ cup butter
½ tablespoon sugar

Filling

2 ounces sweet chocolate
2 8-ounce packages cream cheese
4 eggs
¾ cup sugar
2½ teaspoons instant coffee
dash salt

Combine wafer crumbs, butter, and sugar. Butter sides and bottom of an 8-inch springform pan. Press crumb mixture evenly onto bottom of pan. Melt chocolate over hot, not boiling, water; stir until smooth. Beat cream cheese until smooth. Add eggs to cream cheese, one at a time. Gradually add sugar mixing until well blended. Add melted chocolate, instant coffee and salt; stir until blended. Turn mixture into prepared pan. Bake cake at 350° in center of oven for 40 minutes or until cake center is almost set. It will firm when chilled.

Let cheesecake cool for about 45 minutes. Cover and chill in refrigerator at least 4 hours. Garnish with chocolate or fresh raspberries.

Don Shane is an award-winning broadcaster. Currently the sports anchor and director for WXYZ-TV.

Index

Do you Have an A-Maize-ing recipe?

Here's your chance to share your own Wolverine cuisine with maize and blue fans. All you have to do to be a part of an upcoming installment of A-Maize-ing Tailgating is send us your favorite recipe. Just type it up and send it to *A-Maize-ing Tailgating* c/o Momentum Books, 6964 Crooks Rd., Suite 1, Troy, Michigan 48098.

In case you are wondering, there are several more cookbooks planned. While this volume highlights the players and coaches, volume II will highlight recipes from famous University of Michigan Alumni. Volume III will highlight the delicious recipes from all of you Wolverine fans. So consider this your chance to be a galloping gourmet as well as a supporter of the Millie Schembechler Adrenal Cancer Fund. When you send your recipe make sure you also include a little bit of information about yourself, and your legendary tailgates. If you'd like, please include tailgating pictures. (We will not be able to return them so do not send your only copy.)

Go Blue!

Suzanne, Halle, John and Jake along with Bo at the 1981 Rose Bowl Reunion tailgate party.

About the Author

Suzanne Wangler is an award winning journalist who has spent the past 11 years covering television news for NBC, UPN and CBS affiliates. Suzanne's work has earned her numerous awards including the Associated Press first place award in spot news and investigative reporting, and Michigan Association of Broadcasters award for best feature. Suzanne's investigation into the corruption at the Wayne County Morgue in Detroit earned her a Diamond Award in reporting for Women in Communications.

Currently, she specializes in live reports from WDIV-TV's Chopper 4, the station's high-tech, multi-camera equipped helicopter.

She is married to John Wangler, former University of Michigan football quarterback. They reside in Michigan and have spent many hours preparing Wolverine Cuisine to make tailgating memories even tastier.

If you would like to learn more about the Millie Schembechler Adrenal Cancer Research Fund endowment please write to:

Bo Schembechler
1200 S. State St.
Ann Arbor, MI 48104-3717

If you would like to make additional donations to Millie Schembechler Adrenal Cancer Research Fund, please send your check to:

Millie Schembechler Memorial Foundation
1200 S. State St.
Ann Arbor, MI 48104-3717